INCREASE YOUR SALES THE TACK WAY

Increase your sales the Tack way

Alfred Tack

Gower

First published 1989 by Gower Publishing Company Limited

This paperback edition published 1990 by
Gower Publishing Company Limited
Gower House
Croft Road, Aldershot
Hants GU11 3HR
England

British Library Cataloguing in Publication Data
Tack, Alfred
   Increase your sales the Tack way.
   1. Salesmanship – Manuals
   I. Title
   658.8'5

ISBN 0 566 02878 6

Printed and bound in Great Britain by
Billing & Sons Ltd, Worcester

Contents

Preface

This is a book for all those involved in selling – the embryo salesman, slightly fearful of the new challenge; the experienced, professional salesman, conscious of his status and ever seeking to improve his technique so as to remain a leader; the sales manager seeking new ways to motivate his sales force, and the training manager looking for fresh ideas or seeking a book to use as a training manual.

I have also integrated the Tack story with the teaching material, so you will read how the basic skills of selling helped us to achieve success in areas other than person-to-person selling.

We are often asked the questions: How did you start? What gave you the idea of entering the training field? How did you, as a salesman without capital, build a large organization both in the industrial field and in training? There are many other questions that we are asked, which I hope will be answered in the story of Tack – a story which, in itself, contains many lessons for ambitious salesmen.

But perhaps you will ask a different question when glancing at the chapter headings. Why does the chapter on Getting the Interview appear so late in the book? Surely it should be included earlier. The answer is that all the lessons in the previous chapters on selling apply to getting the interview. Only with this prior knowledge can the problem of obtaining the maximum number of interviews each day be solved.

If you are a woman, you may be asking: Why do you continually refer to 'salesmen' when there are so many successful women in the sales world – that is being sexist! Sorry, it is not meant to be. We employ some three hundred sales women, as well as a highly efficient team of women instructors. Any one of them would be right to demand an explanation – but is there any sensible alternative? To refer continually to 'salesmen or sales women' also jars after a while. So throughout the book I have used the word 'salesmen' in the main, as a generic term to cover both sexes.

I wish all of you every success, and hope that this book will help you to achieve all your sales objectives.

Alfred Tack

1 Thank you, Uncle Joe!

Most people have, on occasion, speculated on how a chain of events began by one simple act. In my case the act occurred when I was seventeen – I met Uncle Joe.

The strategy of Fate is beyond the ken of mankind, but the logical thinker might claim that such acts of chance are allied to opportunities. The chance is not taken – then the opportunity is lost.

The young man sitting by an attractive girl at a party may later marry her, live happily ever after, and claim that one chance visit to a party changed his whole life. The logician might assert that the chance meeting was only an opportunity, which would have been lost by some through nervousness or fear of rebuff.

The meeting was by chance; the outcome was the acceptance of an opportunity by that young man. But let others speculate on the link between seemingly unrelated acts, and the seizing of opportunities. The meeting with Uncle Joe changed my life.

Two days afterwards I had the opportunity of joining a discount bank. I refused. I was already enthused by the concept of success through salesmanship.

I remember Uncle Joe's words as clearly now as on that day which changed my life. To convince me that salesmanship should be my career he said, 'Alfred, you can be a highly successful engineer – accountant – designer – general manager ... but if there were a recession you would be just as likely to be sacked as if you were not doing your job properly, or were below average. The same applies to a below average salesman – but never' – and he repeated, – 'never is an outstanding salesman dismissed for economic reasons. Never is a successful salesman unemployed, even in the worst of recessions. And that applies, world-wide. An outstanding salesman quickly proves his worth!'

I remember Uncle Joe repeating the word 'outstanding' with emphasis, and adding, 'Which means that you must become better than the other salesmen employed in your company'.

Timidly I asked, 'And how is that to be achieved?'

Without hesitation he replied, 'It means being a true professional, and all that that implies'.

I didn't know then what he meant by *professional*, but I do know now.

I can also remember asking him, 'But how do I get a selling job at my age?' I was seventeen, and had been unemployed for six months.

He brushed that problem aside. 'If you're going to worry about trivialities, you'll never succeed as a salesman. Someone will be prepared to throw you in at the deep end, even if they only splash out by rewarding you on straight commission terms.'

The next day I became a salesman on a *no sale – no earn* basis, and I began my understanding of what professional salesmanship meant. A good summing up would be *honest persuasion*.

Cynics may sneer at such triteness, because they have no conception of what honest persuasion means.

From that chance meeting with Uncle Joe began a lifetime of earning a living by satisfying customer needs. My brother and I now control a diversified group of companies, including an air-conditioning division with a highly computerised factory in South Wales, employing some twenty highly skilled technical salesmen calling on contractors, architects, and surveyors; a hygiene division and a pest control division, employing some 300 sales staff, selling direct to factories, offices, and shops, as well as through retail outlets; and a printing company, with a high reputation for the quality of its work, employing a small but specialised salesforce. Tack Training International and Tack Management Consultants employ some thirty salesmen, who are also training and consultancy advisers. Tack Training International has twenty-six associate companies throughout the world, covering over forty-four countries, and each company employs its own salesforce.

Such statistics are always boring, but I felt you should know that not only do we teach salesmanship, but we also practise successfully what we teach.

Obviously I am not claiming that our success is due solely to our being able to outsell our competitors, but it is one of the reasons for our becoming leaders in our respective fields. Another reason is our insistence on *quality* throughout our organisation, whether it be in the reception area, the sales offices, accounts department, service department, or on the production lines.

Brian Moss, the managing director of our industrial divisions, was recently awarded the OBE for his work in promoting quality control throughout British Industry.

But more about that ingredient for success later. Back now to my first selling job.

My father had highly placed contacts in the City, which implies that he was a banker or an insurance tycoon. Not at all! He was a tobacconist, with a shop in St Michael's Alley, a turning off Cornhill.

One of the claims to fame of my father's shop was that it was adjacent to *The George and Vulture* public house, made famous by Charles Dickens in *Pickwick Papers*. The Pickwick Club originated there. In addition, the shop was in the midst of London's financial centre. It was not like most tobacconist's shops of today, selling newspapers, sweets, childrens' toys, etc. My father blended his own pipe tobacco, and advised the great City bankers on which cigars to choose for that important luncheon, or as a gift at Christmas time. His shop was a City institution, frequented by the City aristocracy.

I had left school without any academic qualifications. I don't think my masters had thought it worth their while to continue to try teaching someone whose mind was always on other matters. When I left at sixteen and a half, my father felt certain that he would have no problem in getting me a job with a bank, discount house, insurance company, or some other financial institution. His optimism, much to the annoyance of my mother, was ill-founded. Dad may have been a famous cigar merchant – maybe chairmen and managing directors appreciated his great knowledge of cigars – but that didn't mean that they were willing to grant his son, who was without qualifications, some special favour. In those days school leavers received no government handouts, so I was hard up and in low spirits when I bumped into Uncle Joe after leaving my father's shop.

Uncle Joe at that time was an agent for a Swiss company in the embroidery/trimmings field. He had been selling for years, and if he had not spent each week far more than he earned – high as were his earnings – he would have been a rich man, according to my father. When therefore I told him of Uncle Joe's advice, I had expected that he would be highly critical of the suggestion that I should become a salesman. I believed that he was keen to make me a banker or an insurance magnate.

Perhaps he realised by that time that, possibly, I was not cut out for such prestigious positions.

'Right!' he said, 'I can give you your first job'.

'Behind the counter?' I asked dismally. I had always disliked that idea, which had been mooted previously.

'No,' he replied, 'you can enrol members for our association'.

My father seemed to believe that his brother Joe's idea that I should make a career in selling had in some way turned me instantaneously into a super-salesman!

Dad had been helping to form a new association for retail tobacconists, to take over from the old association to which most tobacconists then belonged. Many tobacconists believed that the old association was out of touch with prevailing conditions. These included cut-price tobacconist shops, and the newly arrived cigarette machines beginning to appear outside butchers, bakers, and the proverbial candlestick-makers. Most of the bona fide tobacconists wanted to close down such outlets, and this was the objective of the new association – but it only had about twenty members. At a meeting of the committee a resolution had been passed that all members of the committee should make a point of trying to increase membership. My father didn't fancy that idea at all, and he delegated the job to me, on a 10 per cent commission basis.

Without any training, guidance or advice, except that given in a very inexpensive leaflet, I began my career as a salesman and suddenly, for some inexplicable reason, I was being hailed by the family as *a born salesman*. It took me many years to realise the nonsense of that statement!

Some people may be born with attributes which might later be helpful in this sphere – good health, a pleasing appearance, articulacy – but none of these assets lead to certain success as a salesman. Salesmen become successful either through their own experience over many years or by training.

But the label born salesman was attached to me at that time. A better description would have been a petrified salesman. I was scared stiff at the thought of making my first call.

I lived at that time in a house in Chiswick, about eight miles from Central London, with my parents, brothers, and sister. On the day I started my career I did what most novices, as well as some experienced salesmen, do regularly: to make my first call I travelled some four miles to Shepherds Bush.

Why travel four miles, when there were so many tobacconists in Chiswick High Street, or thereabouts? The answer was to delay the inevitable moment of truth when that first prospect had to be faced. Of course that lesson was only driven home some time afterwards, but it didn't take me long to become aware that mostly, we can generate our own time-wasting activities, because we *want* to waste time. It's as simple as that! And no time-management system will effect a complete cure. It is all a question of self-discipline.

Life's tough, isn't it! Instead of arriving at a tobacconist's shop therefore at 8.30, I delayed my first attempt until nearer 9.30. And even then, I didn't make my call on the first tobacconist I saw.

I viewed the shop from the other side of the street, didn't like the look of it, crossed the road and walked past it. I retraced my steps, passed it again, then made up my mind that it didn't look grand enough for the owner to want to join our new Tobacconists' Association.

Eventually, I made my first call.

It was a disaster, and the hurt of that call is almost as searing now as it was that day.

The owner of the shop, as is statutory, had his name displayed over the door as licensee to sell tobacco. Walking timidly inside the shop, I saw a rotund, balding man standing there, and in a questioning manner said, 'Mr Livingstone?'

He responded, 'Yes, and if you're Stanley I don't want to be discovered!'

He must have used that gag many, many times, and

enjoyed telling his friends of his cutting response to a salesman's questioning approach.

Lost for words, I turned and almost ran out of the shop.

I had not walked more than a few paces before, to my great joy, I found myself standing outside a teashop. There were many of them in those days, quiet, clean, happy places, not to be compared with today's fast-food eateries. I had coffee and a Bath bun, a bad habit which I acquired then and which lasted a long, long time. I would often spend half an hour or so at the best time of the day looking for a teashop rather than a prospect. Eventually I learned something which is now taught as standard on our territory management course: Selling time wasted can never be recaptured, and mid-morning is a key selling time. But perhaps I learned something else from that call on Mr Livingstone. Possibly it was the beginning of a train of thought which led to my giving, in my first book on salesmanship, published in 1950, some ten forms of arousing interest at the approach stage, all without risk of embarrassment.

Luckily I was born with one asset: an intense dislike of being beaten. At school we were taught to be good losers. Fine! But there's no real difference between being a good falsely smiling loser and an inwardly seething loser.

All salesman have to take rebuff after rebuff from prickly buyers, sarcastic buyers, super-snob buyers, overworked buyers ... But after years of buffeting the skin does become thicker.

However, good training can often obviate such rebuffs.

After the Livingstone episode I decided to explain my mission to the first person I met inside a shop, regardless of whether he was the owner or not. However, I found that didn't work at all, so I returned once more to approaching a person by the name over the door; and that is what we are teaching in our courses to-day – *always try to find the name of the buyer in advance*.

It was during these early days that I worked out my first approach sentence. It was, 'Are you satisfied with the help you are getting from your trade association?'

The question approach is standard these days, but I thought I was being most original – and it worked then, as it does today. The answer from the tobacconist was nearly always 'No'. After all, few in any sphere of business activity really appreciate the work of their trade association. Most people feel the association could do more to help the members.

The first time I used that approach resulted in the tobacconist joining our association. What elation – pride – joy . . .!

Quickly, however, I learned the vicissitudes of selling, and to make the most of the good days to counterbalance those which were not so good. I do remember that after that first sale, which was in the afternoon, I telephoned home to announce my success. It was as though my fortune had been made. In fact I had earned one pound.

On hearing the news, my mother prepared a special celebration meal for the occasion – and my mother's special meals could put on fourteen pounds at a sitting!

Uncle Joe was invited. Even my father, not given to emotion, smiled knowingly, indicating that all along he had known that I should make a first-class salesman rather than a banker.

The family was idiotically certain that Uncle Joe had helped to create a selling genius – and all that after one sale!

Personally I did not feel nearly so optimistic, and I would much rather not have met Uncle Joe but have become an embryo banker.

Most salesmen go through this time of anxiety and stress, but it soon passes. As time progressed, I became more confident, and within two weeks I had enrolled ten new members – something of a record. The previous record of any committee member's achievement had been two enrolments. In spite of my activities, the association collapsed. It decided it could not afford to carry on and fight battles on behalf of tobacconists who were mostly members of another association.

Once more I was out of work, but my fame had spread throughout the family. Another of my father's brothers, Uncle Mick, was a manufacturer of ladies' knitwear. He had been in partnership with a friend. The friend was the salesman and my uncle was the production manager. They had split up for various reasons, the main one being that each of the wives thought her husband was doing all the work and therefore should receive more pay. Uncle Mick started on his own after the break-up, only to discover that, although he could produce a good range of knitwear, he couldn't sell it. This created another problem. Being under-funded or, more realistically, almost broke, Uncle Mick couldn't afford to employ a salesman. Imagine the state he was in, that he was pleased to offer me the job at £1 a week and commission! I was the straw he was clutching at. I accepted the offer, but, knowing little about knitwear, asked to be allowed to spend the first week at the factory, which was rather a large shed, and not my idea of a factory at all. Reluctantly Uncle Mick agreed to this product training. He held the belief that a fully experienced salesman like me should be able to sell anything.

Times haven't changed, have they? That belief is still held today by so many executives, who consider that product training is covered by a quick walk around the factory. Too many salesmen are sent out with too little product knowledge.

Although the management is to blame, salesmen with the right mental attitude will soon discover ways and means of improving their product knowledge rather than giving way to despair at walking around a factory accompanied by some disinterested person.

My teacher was Florrie Dallender, a lovely lady who unfortunately knew nothing about the art of teaching. And she was very deaf.

There were two outstanding aspects of Uncle Mick's knitwear, of which he was very proud. There was the silk plating (whatever that meant) and fully-fashioning (which I didn't understand, either)! I did not therefore start off with a great deal of product knowledge, but I did learn several lessons from my experience in selling knitwear to retail outlets which have been incorporated in our courses.

The first, naturally, was the necessity of teaching product knowledge through offer analysis.

The second was that a salesman with a large case of samples, calling for an appointment, should leave that case behind and only take with him one or two items, whatever he is selling.

Calling on Selfridge's, I joined the queue of salesmen waiting to see the knitwear buyer. She had never given me an interview: it was always 'Nothing today', via an assistant.

My green fibre case, so large it held the best part of our range of knitwear, was called the Green Monster. Weightlifters could have used it for muscle-building exercises.

I made my fifth call at Selfridges', when once more the assistant walked towards me, asked for my card and very speedily returned with the standard 'Nothing today'. By that time I knew the buyer well by sight, but mistakenly doubted that she was even aware of my existence. True, she didn't know me, but she did know the Green Monster.

Seeing how dejected I looked on hearing the inevitable, an elderly salesman – he must have been all of forty, but in those days that was very elderly to me – said, 'No luck?'

'Fraid not!'

'May I suggest a reason?'

'Go ahead! But how can she keep saying "Nothing today" when she doesn't even know what I have in my case?'

'I think that's your problem, the case. Haven't you got a car?'

'No!'

'You carry that thing everywhere?'

'Yes.'

'You must be a hero! Most reps in our field have a car, and if they haven't got an appointment to show their full range, they leave their case in the car and carry one or two items over their arm – numbers that they believe are winners. Buyers and their assistants notice a case like yours. They know that time will be wasted by having to look through a whole range when they can tell from a sample whether they are interested or not. No buyer wants to be landed with a salesman, working possibly for a company unknown to her, who has a case like yours which, when opened, will result in garments littering the floor and desk – and knowing that she will even have to wait while they are repacked.

'Get rid of that bag and you'll get your interviews.'

It was good advice.

At my next call I put the case in the left-luggage office, taking with me only a couple of samples. It worked. I was seen, and I got an order. I asked if I could show her the whole range and she replied, 'Not now', then made an appointment for me to see her with the full range a couple of weeks later.

So the lesson is: *Don't scare buyers off with the size of your sample bag or demonstration unit.* You first have to get their interest in one or two of your best sellers. In any event, at this interview too many samples only cause conflict in the mind of the buyer.

This advice has been given to many salesmen, in many different fields, and subsequently they have obtained interviews where previously they had been told, 'Nothing today!'

Lesson three occurred when I called on a male buyer of knitwear at Jays', the one-time famous Regent Street store. They received no sympathy from me when they closed down; I felt it served them right. I should not have been so vindictive against a company because of the misdemeanours of one person, the buyer, but he ruined my day, my week almost my sales career. And yet he was in the right.

But it is how one person justifies righteousness that is all important.

Following my usual procedure, standing with my samples over my arm, I was told by an assistant that the great man would see me. Confidently I approached 'His Lordship'.

Brusquely he said, 'I don't know your company. How long have they been in existence?', and before waiting for my reply he went on, 'And to save my time you should know that I am only interested in the top end of the market'.

I went off at a gallop, explaining how the company had originated, the quality of its range, and muttering something about plated knitting, fully-fashioning, and the brilliance of the designer. The only thing I didn't tell him was that the designer was my Uncle Mick.

He listened for a while, then interrupted, 'What on earth are you gabbling about?'

I stopped, hesitated, then became an inert mass of flesh. The great man left me to speak to an assistant. I picked up my samples and almost sleep-walked out of Jays', never to return.

But that buyer was right, even if he did lack even the slightest conception of human relations or compassion. I made straight for my favourite teashop at the top end of Oxford Street, and consoled myself with coffee and a Bath bun.

I knew I was so right at that time, and that he was a So-and-so So-and-so So-and-so. . .

But I was wrong. This lesson should be memorised by every salesman. Salesmen are usually exuberant and enthusiastic people, whose outlet is very often a torrent of words; but a priority of all salesmen is to be understood – to be able to communicate effectively. The buyer or prospective buyer should not be expected to decipher messages from the spill-out of an over-wrought mind.

Without being boring, every salesman should speak slowly. All golfing instructors give the advice, 'Swing slowly; and however slowly you think you are swinging, just swing a bit slower!' But although you will talk slowly, you will still use emphasis, good enunciation . . . You will not murmur or mumble, and you will make sure that every sentence is understood.

Check up on yourself for the next week, and be honest with your answers.

Jay's buyer did help me to learn that lesson, but it didn't dawn on me as quickly as that. It was not as though a shaft of understanding had flashed from the subconscious, to penetrate my conscious mind. Gradually I realised that I had to curb my impetuosity, and my tongue.

You do the same, if you have that 'gabbling' tendency. I still haven't quite mastered that lesson, but I do my best. All you can do is your best. I know how hard it is, when enthusiasm takes over, to talk slowly but emphatically.

Remember, if you cannot communicate well, you cannot sell well.

I tried to learn not to talk too slowly, but not to sprint through the presentation; not to shout, but not to whisper . . .

It didn't take me many more weeks to decide that the coffees and Bath buns were taking quite a sizeable slice out of my best selling time. It took a great deal of self-discipline to cut out the break.

Life, as you know, has its compensations. On the same day as the Jays' buyer sapped my confidence I met a buyer who partly restored it – although it was not fully restored for some weeks. She was Miss Rogers, the knitwear buyer at the Oxford Street branch of the giant Dutch C & A complex.

Because they had no left-luggage office, I lugged my green monster with me, then hid it behind a rail of dresses after extracting two models. By some chance there was no queue of salesmen that morning waiting to see Miss Rogers. She noticed me but, unlike the buyer at Selfridges', Miss Rogers herself came towards me. A diminutive, sweet lady, she said, 'Who do you represent?'

I told her. She had never heard of us, but she invited me to bring my samples to the far end of the department, where there was a table. I then blurted out that actually I had left my case behind the dress rail. She told me to collect it, picked out three numbers, and ordered six of each – a massive order for me, at that time. I could have hugged her.

She said, 'Have you just started?'

I hesitated, then answered truthfully, 'Yes'. I had been told by my uncle never to make that admission, as buyers do not appreciate the worth of a new, unknowledgeable salesman.

Miss Rogers said, 'You look so worried – you shouldn't be! You have a good, saleable range. Be more confident in yourself, and you'll win through'.

She had obviously sympathised with my youthfulness, although this had antagonised the Jays' tyrant.

Sometimes I think that my concern with human relations began with my meeting with these two buyers, the first with no knowledge of how to motivate people, though salesmen, when well motivated, can so often go out of their way to help buyers. Miss Rogers, on the other hand, was a 'natural' so far as human relations were concerned. She was a good friend to me for some while afterwards.

I have not coloured the truth. I have related exactly what happened. At times when things go wrong, we need someone to restore our faith in ourselves and humanity. You will have early problems, and later problems, because salesmen have problems most of the time, but perhaps my early experiences will help you to keep your confidence high, while overcoming the hurdles every salesman meets on so many days of his selling life.

Just one more lesson from those early days of selling knitwear. In the same way as I could never get interviews at Selfridge's, so I could never get an interview at Bourne & Hollingsworth, although for very different reasons. Bourne & Hollingsworth was a world famous store in Oxford Street, which has since been taken over completely, changed and changed again, but the famous name is one which readily comes to the mind of anyone who has ever been connected with retail stores.

Bourne & Hollingsworth had a different buying policy from other stores. It had buying rooms. No salesman was allowed to see a buyer in a department, except by special invitation. In the buying room there was a central area, surrounded by chairs in which the salesmen sat waiting for the return of the commissionaire who had collected their card to take to the buyer, and return with the news, 'The buyer will come down to see you', or 'The buyer is not interested'.

So many salesmen seemed to be receiving the good news, while after some ten visits I had yet to be allowed to see the buyer. How I envied those salesmen whose cards were not returned, and who were later warmly greeted by a buyer, and ushered into one of the small buying rooms alongside the main area.

On the eleventh call, which proved again to be 'Not today!', I had had enough. I left the Green Monster in one of the buying rooms when the commissionaire wasn't looking, took out a couple of samples, left the buying room, which was adjacent to the side entrance to Bourne & Hollingsworth, made for the main entrance, walked up the stairs to the first floor and into the knitwear department.

As soon as I was spotted by an assistant, and assistants can recognise salesmen a long way away, she hurried across, eyebrows raised in a severe questioning look. 'Can I help you?' she asked, not in any way intending to help me at all.

'Yes, I want to see Miss Lawrence.'

'Are you a representative?'

'Yes.'

'I'm afraid you have broken one of the company's rules. If you go downstairs and make for the side entrance you will find our buying rooms, and –'

'I've been into that buying room ten times', I interrupted, 'and I've always received a "Not today thank you" response!'

A voice said in a loud tone, 'What is it, Marcia?' The voice emanated from a middle-aged lady, standing by a display of knitwear. I guessed she must be Miss Lawrence, the buyer.

I faced a challenge. Should I walk away or accept it? I accepted, approached the buyer. 'Miss Lawrence', I said, 'please can you help me?'

Much later those magic words *Can you help me?* have been emphasised in all my books. Very few people will answer negatively. Most will be rather pleased to feel that their assistance has been sought.

But the words must be spoken in a pleasant manner, neither bombastically nor servilely, just the way you would ask someone for directions if you were lost in a new town.

Miss Lawrence was about to move away but hesitated, so I repeated, 'Miss Lawrence, please can you help me?'

'In which way?' she asked coldly.

'I have been to the buying room ten times. My company won't believe this. On each occasion on sending through my card to your department I have received the reply, 'Not today'. Will you please make an exception to the rule and look at some of my suits?' Again my youth, and ignorance of protocol, won the day.

She said, 'It is a firm rule of the company that we are only allowed to buy from specified suppliers, and your company is not one of our specified suppliers'.

'But how do I become a specified supplier if no one will look at my range?'

She smiled. 'I see your point of view – it is one we have discussed. Let me see what you have.'

She examined my sample, then told me to return to the buying room and she would come down to see me later. When 'later' arrived, she gave me a small order, promising repeats if it sold well.

From that day onwards my confidence never again wavered. As mentioned before, in every career there are turning points – some minor, some decisive. Breaking the Bourne & Hollingsworth rule was a decisive one for me.

I was proud of myself. I felt that Everest had been conquered. A strength born in me then did not fade away under duress. That call must be allied to the one I made on Miss Rogers at C & A. It was a joint effort which really sent my confidence sky high.

The world is full of people who are continually

exclaiming, 'Oh, you can't do that! You can't call before nine o'clock in the morning – no one will see you. You can't telephone him direct – you'll never get through to him. You can't get him to come to the factory, he's far too busy. You can never get in without an appointment . . .'

Don't be a 'can't-er'. Be different. Accept every challenge, however preposterous it may seem. You will be surprised at what you can achieve when you take action while others are complaining, and doing nothing.

I hope the lesson I learned at Bourne & Hollingsworth will benefit you. Just stop reading and think about it for a moment. Although so much happened, at that time I was learning the craft of salesmanship – never of knitwear. After twelve months my uncle's company had achieved some success. It was profitable. He decided to sell out, and he retired.

I was retired as well, but Uncle Joe was right again. If you achieve a measure of success in selling, there is no trouble in getting a job. I had brief spells in advertising, office supplies, and carnival novelties. During this period Brother George was an apprentice engineer.

For someone like me, who doesn't understand the complexities of a tap washer, he seemed on a par with Stevenson and his Rocket. I suggested to him that he should design and make something, and I would sell it. That 'something' arrived in the shape of a sunshade-cum-umbrella – not exactly a precision engineering job!

We had both seen a picture in a foreign publication showing a beautiful girl sunbathing while protected from the sun's burning rays by a see-through sunshade. We thought that was a winning idea, and could visualise thousands of such sunshades being used on beaches throughout the world.

After some very minor research we decided that the material should be a type of clear plastic film, which had been used for a number of years as wrapping paper. There were then no see-through plastic materials, as there are to-day.

In conjunction with the experience of an elderly manufacturer we eventually produced the first see-through sunshade-cum-umbrella. Our showcard depicted a gorgeous girl relaxing on a beach, her delicate fair skin protected from the sun's rays by the *Solette* – the name we gave our invention. With sample in hand, my first call was at Selfridge's

I opened up the sunshade as if to inspect it as soon as I arrived in the umbrella department. Yes, showmanship was always a part of selling!

To cut a long story short, the buyers everywhere almost fell over themselves to stock our *Solettes*, some almost pleading for sole rights. It was simply great, being in that position – the only time in my life it has ever occurred. Brilliant salesmanship was not needed. We were soon inundated with orders. We delivered quickly, and then, some few weeks later, we became inundated again – with complaints!

The clear film, unlike today's plastics, could not be satisfactorily stitched – the stitching always split away. The film had to be stitched to the frame as well as to the main umbrella support handle. The conclusion was that after the sunshade had been used a few times the film split away from the frame.

Another lesson had been learned – and a very expensive lesson. Never again did we make the mistake of not testing to destruction.

Later, when George invented one of the first coin-operated automatic vending machines – up until then such machines had always had pull out drawers – he used a relay of people to insert coins continuously, to make sure that the automatic device operated under the worst possible conditions, and also that the coin mechanisms didn't jam.

We lost our savings in the *Solette* operation, and were determined from then on to sell only high quality products. To succeed, a salesman must have faith in the quality, irrespective of the price of the product he is selling.

We had to take back the faulty *Solettes*, and so lost heavily. All our savings disappeared, and we had to get jobs. Both of us were then married – to sisters, incidentally – and we had to make a good living fast.

We joined a company marketing cigarette-vending machines, on straight commission terms. The company was founded by a Dane – Find Graucob. We sold well, broke records, achieved promotion, and some eighteen months later, incredible as it may seem, we became the joint controllers of that company, employing well over 100 salesmen, eight area managers and a sales manager.

It was soon afterwards that George invented the automatic vending machine. Later the company bought NuSwift, the fire-fighting organization, and we became directors of that company. But we had long decided that we wanted to start our own company. Although we had regained some capital, it was not enough to venture into a new field, and many companies fail through lack of capital or cash flow.

There is always a moan from managers today when we circulate one of our cost-cutting memos. Our obsession with cost-cutting began when we started another business on our own account. Our managers now need only sanction a payment and a cheque is made out, but in those days we first had to make sure that there was enough money in the bank to meet the cheque.

This was how we started our own business. One day a salesman who had once worked for us called in, as he put it, for old time's sake. That always means that the salesman has done well and wants to prove the foolishness of those who let him go, or else he is not doing so well, and would like to be re-engaged.

This salesman told us that he was doing very well, selling air-conditioning units.

That was our lucky day!

Don't you agree that so many people, faced with the same situation, would have let the salesman's success story waft over their heads and away from them? We didn't! We listened, asked questions, and were intrigued with the possibilities in the heating, ventilating and air-conditioning field. After much research, we knew exactly what we wanted.

We persuaded Kelvinator, the refrigerator manufacturers, to make us some small portable units which would clean, deodorise, purify, and freshen the air, but not at that stage provide refrigerated air, because of the cost of servicing. To overcome our financial problems we suggested to Graucob that he should finance the new venture, for a half share, but we should have the controlling shares, and have the right to buy him out at a later date.

The new unit was to be called the *Moloniser* and was an instant success. My brother and I did all the selling in the early days, but quickly we built up a salesforce, and added to the range with extractor fans, heaters, and ozonisers. We then took over the complete output of another company manufacturing fans, heaters, etc.

Our training courses for new intakes of salesmen were so advanced for that time that sales executives of many leading organisations asked us to allow them or their managers to attend, and to learn more about our training methods. Remember training was then in its infancy.

But the pressure on us to allow others to attend our courses increased because of the publicity we were receiving at that time in the national press and magazines. We always insisted in these articles that our success was due not only to manufacturing excellent products of high quality, but to our sales training. We grew quickly, and were soon employing over 100 salesmen.

We were the pioneers of incentive schemes, which included holidays abroad, cruising, cars, clothes, and domestic appliances. Today such prizes are commonplace, but at that time we had this field to ourselves, resulting in ever-increasing publicity.

We were working six, sometimes seven, days a week. I wrote *Sell Your Way to Success*, which eventually went into eight editions and sold some 300,000 copies. That was one of the factors leading to the setting up of our training organisation. A demand for training existed, that was obvious. We decided to meet that demand.

Again my brother and I did all the selling in those early days. Graucob then decided to devote all his time to NuSwift, and we decided that we didn't want any part of that. We wanted to concentrate on our air-conditioning company, so, as arranged under the agreement we had signed, we bought Graucob's half of the business from him. We had no problem in finding the cash because so many of our friends and associates wanted to invest in our new company.

We formed *Tack AirConditioning Ltd*, which later became *NuAire Ltd*. In 1948 we also formed *Tack Tuition Ltd*, which has now become *Tack Training International Ltd*.

Our success saga has continued, with all our companies being leaders in their respective spheres of activity.

Thank you, Uncle Joe!

2   Proud to be a salesman

Buyers from all over the world do not queue at our doors to spend their millions with us. Every single product, service, intangible ... contributing to this massive sum has to be sold by a salesman. Most people do not equate these outstanding achievements with the film and TV coverage of salesmanship, where salesmen are mostly depicted as desk-thumping extroverts, seedy down-at-heel bores, or high-pressure con men, persuading pensioners and newlyweds to part with their cash for time-share apartments overseas, home improvements, or quack remedies – sheer libel on a group of people to whom so many owe a living!

But these parodies of salesmanship have an effect on the salesmen themselves, and on their families. Often salesmen's wives or husbands cover up when asked what their spouses do for a living. They will say, 'He's a technical adviser', – 'a consultant' – 'she's in advertising' – 'he's in books' – or 'she works for a fire protection authority' ... in an attempt to disguise the truth.

Proudly they should say, 'My partner is a salesman!'

Why do TV exposure programmes concentrate on a tiny minority of door-to-door salesmen whose code of conduct is suspect? It is for the usual reason – the bad is always much better copy or viewing than the good. What a pity they take this point of view, because most salesmen are honest people employed by reputable companies selling good products and services!

Within our own group we have a team of export salesmen selling our air-conditioning equipment all over the world, and especially in the Middle East. Can anyone imagine that such men or women could succeed by using unethical practices? Looking at TV soap operas or investigative programmes, one would hardly credit that outstanding men and women are selling forklift trucks, computers, airplanes, ships, office equipment, buildings ... They succeed by keeping to sound selling and negotiating principles; but to the general public all salesmen are foot-in-the-door, high-pressure bulldozers.

Only we, as salesmen, can put things right, by being proud of our calling and telling all our friends and relations exactly what we do.

Some people criticise high-pressure selling when they haven't the slightest idea of what high pressure means. In fact it doesn't exist. High-pressure selling is only another name for fraudulent selling, which still only applies, as I have already said, to a very tiny minority of door-to-door salesmen.

In all other fields such selling doesn't apply, because purchasing is carried out by professional or semi-professional buyers. For example, to attempt to pressurise a purchasing officer employed by a government department, store, hospital, etc., or to try to force a buyer to purchase against his or her will or judgement, will lead to the salesman being ordered out of the premises very quickly.

If a salesman were to make misleading statements which a professional buyer did happen to accept, that order would very quickly be cancelled or the products returned after delivery. Even the owner of that corner shop or small garage is used to dealing with salesmen, and will rarely be coerced against his will or judgement to place an order for products or services which will not benefit his business.

So once again, be proud of your calling, and remember that there are only a few dishonest salesmen – just as there are a few dishonest doctors, lawyers, City merchants, and even some ministers of the Church who run off with someone else's wife. But no one in their right mind condemns the Church, the accountancy or law institutes, for the misdemeanours of the few.

So remember, from now on there is no need to call yourself an 'industrial negotiator', an 'executive representative', or even just a 'sales engineer'. Keep repeating the words *I am a salesman*, and when you say them, see that you have a glint in your eye, a firmness of the chin . . .

When I got that first job selling membership of a tobacconists' association, I remember meeting a schoolfriend in the street one day. He said, 'What do you do?' and happily I replied, 'I am a salesman!'

As a company, we have fought hard for the rights of salesmen over many years. We have also fought hard to upgrade salesmanship in the eyes of the general public. Join us in our fight to win the respect for salesmanship that it deserves.

Emerson's belief that if you build a better mousetrap buyers will queue at your door is no longer true. There has to be a well-trained sales force to sell that super mousetrap before production begins; otherwise failure is certain.

In the USA a few years back multi-nationals in the fast-moving consumer field decided that the public flocked into the shops for their products because of massive advertising campaigns, so they decided to cut down their salesforces. Within twelve months they realised that they had made a mistake, and the sales forces were rebuilt.

That will give you some idea of why Britain depends so much on good salesmanship, both at home and overseas.

Nothing happens until something is sold is an old tag. Maybe it's an idea – maybe it's a plan – but more likely, it's a product or service which leads to the creation of more goods.

A salesman is a job creator.

3 The right mental attitude

'Monday, bloody Monday!' were the words used by Stewart Murray, who retired recently as managing director of TACK Training International, when opening a sales-training course. Then, pausing for effect, he would smile broadly, straighten his back and say, 'That didn't impress you as an opening to the course, did it? But I was only acting out the thoughts of so many salesmen on Monday morning'.

Perhaps they'd had a bad weekend – there was no picnic due to bad weather, the children were miserable, the refrigerator had broken down – and as so often happens on a Monday, the rain pours down, and all the salesman can think of is meeting that belligerent buyer, or the receptionist who on four previous occasions has barred his way with the words, 'I'm sorry, he's busy'. So, to many salesmen, it is 'Monday, bloody Monday!', and the week gets off to a bad start.

Stewart, now sailing his yacht around the Isle of Wight, enjoys his retirement, but we still miss his infectious enthusiasm, and remember his constant stressing to salesmen that you cannot succeed unless you have the *right mental attitude*. That possibly means persuading you to change your thinking pattern, so that you will have the right mental attitude towards learning to adapt and accept change.

Over the years many hundreds of salesmen call on us for advice. Often it concerns their dissatisfaction with their present employers, and the need to find a new job. An early question is, 'Why do you want to leave your present company – why did you leave your last company?' Not one – I repeat, not one – has ever answered, 'I didn't try hard enough', 'I got into a rut' or 'I wasn't amenable to new ideas'. The replies vary between 'The company didn't give me enough backing', 'They didn't keep their promises', 'They can't compete', 'Without advertising it was impossible to succeed', 'They didn't keep stocks', 'It was impossible to get on with the sales manager', 'They're too small', 'They haven't got the cash' and 'They're too large and impersonal'. But surely *all* those companies couldn't have been *all* that bad! When a firm has been in existence for any length of time, someone must have sold its products well. What is so rarely realised is that there are snags with every company.

When a salesman applies for a position and is granted an interview, he will answer a strong 'Yes' to such questions as, *Are you a dedicated hard worker? Are you a self-starter? Are you a self-motivator?* But are these answers always true?

Conversely, the interviewer will claim that his company is so good to work for that it almost brings tears to the interviewer's eyes as he explains its kindness and generosity – also not always strictly true, either!

The interviewer doesn't explain that the sales manager is too tough, too weak, too old-fashioned or too *avant-garde*. Why should he? There are no perfect employers, anyway. A salesman with the right mental attitude accepts such statements and such snags as being inevitable, but on joining the company he does not then bemoan his fate. He knows that his success will depend on his own skills, and no one at head office can take those skills away from him.

The right mental attitude means the ability to understand the exaggerations of some interviewers and to appreciate that he/she, is also sometimes making exaggerated claims. No salesman should leave a company for another if he is failing. He should only leave on a high note, when he is doing well but wants to do better.

Usually, if a salesman is working for a good company, or even an average company, selling products or services which are value for money, but his sales are not high enough and promotions do not occur, it is the salesman's own mental attitude which is at fault – and this includes his attitude to improving his selling skills. In most companies there are several outstanding salesmen, although not outstanding enough in an all-round way to warrant promotion. By outstanding I do not mean simply reaching sales targets or beating them. I mean making that extra effort day in and day out, so that the extra effort is recognised.

For example, if a memo arrives from the sales manager reading, 'Please push Y, we are overstocked with this unit', the response of many a top salesman is, 'They can stuff Y – I'm not pushing it!' Or the memo may read, 'We must increase the sales of our more profitable lines'. Again the response may be, 'Not me! I'm doing well enough with the lower end of the range'.

A sales manager may instigate special drives: Opening New Account Month, Credit Sales Month, Research Month, or Helping Our Export Drive Month. Again some salesmen, brilliant as they may be but having the wrong mental attitudes, will ignore such requests and then in later years wonder why they have been passed over when a vacancy arises for a regional or area manager.

Let us consider some other aspects of RMA. Reports from salesmen were analysed over a twelve-month period, and here is a list of the number of times various excuses for lack of sales were highlighted:

Due to slump	86
Workers on short time	50
Christmas holiday	140
Summer holiday	70
Easter holiday	35
Taxation due in January	176
No money about	66

Here is the pay-off line: that analysis was carried out in 1936. Salesmen were making the same excuses then as some make now. Some had the wrong mental attitude then, and some have the wrong mental attitude now.

Don't make excuses. Don't look for them. Work out how seeming setbacks can be overcome. Possibly more calls should be made, reassessments of how areas should be worked made so that time can be saved, more positive thinking...

Let others make the excuses. You set out to win. Winning always bring with it a measure of happiness.

RMA applies also to sport. England and Middlesex Captain Mike Gatting said of one of the stalwarts of the Middlesex team, Clive Radley, 'Radders has never been the most talented batsman in the game, but he has more than made up for it by determination, courage, and an ability to improvise.' Sometimes even skills play second fiddle to the right mental attitude.

Have I made my case? I hope so. Only if you have the RMA, can the rest of the book be of benefit to you.

Back in time

After the standstill during the war we restarted in 1945 by engaging salesmen for our reformed unit air-conditioning division.

The five salesmen who attended the first course we held established a record. They were not only each of them outstandingly successful as salesmen, but each played a great part in the growth of our company. They showed us the direction our future should take.

They were:

Bill Logan from Liverpool, later to become the first manager in charge of our new ventilating plant division, formed to sell industrial equipment rather than the small units which had until then been our only products.

Fred Boyes from Leeds, who became a regional director, and when we decided to make a management buyout, offered us all his savings to buy shares in the new company.

Chris Heyworth of Blackburn, later to become known to everyone in the organisation as Uncle Chris, was the first of our field sales managers.

Bob Robinson of Leicester, who later became a Midlands director.

Charlie Briars, who was perhaps the best salesman of all. On his first day out after leaving our training course he sold eighteen units, and he kept up that kind of pace until he retired.

I appreciate that the deeds of such star salesmen are of little interest to you, unless you can benefit from learning something of their achievements. There are lessons in RMA to be learned from each of them.

Imagine you were selling a range of small fans, air purifiers and deodorising units direct to offices and factories. Very little technique was required to sell them. Then suddenly you were faced with a new challenge. Your company has taken over the marketing of a company manufacturing highly technical air-conditioning plant. The buyers of such plant, unlike those who buy small ventilating units and fans, are usually qualified engineers, fully conversant with air movements, humidification, dehumidification, refrigeration, heat losses, etc. What would your reaction be on hearing that your company had entered this highly technical field? Would it be, 'That's not for me!' or 'Now this is a grand new challenge?'

When we made that challenge, the salesforce as a whole were not greatly interested – 'Too difficult!', 'Too technical!', etc. But Bill Logan had the RMA. He enrolled on a course for ventilating engineers, studied hard, read every book he could find on the subject, and visited the factory as often as he could to obtain more information from the technical boffins. He then asked to be allowed to take over the sales of ventilating systems in the North West of the country.

Logan quickly obtained contracts which by today's values would be in the region of a quarter of a million pounds or more. Of course he had the assistance of the factory's technical staff, but Logan had to make the initial call and to win over the engineers responsible for placing the orders. He had to make the first suggestions for a new plant – how it could be installed, what the alterations would entail . . . He also had to persuade the engineers to place their trust in a company which at that time was virtually unknown in the full air-conditioning field.

Logan became a successful manager of our Ventilation Division, a position which was much envied by some who had been with the company longer than he, but who were not willing to change their mental attitude, and pay a price for such success. They wanted others to do for them what they should be doing for themselves.

The lesson to be learned is: *Always accept a new challenge*.

The next lesson is one I have long remembered. It concerns the right mental attitude as applied to health.

It isn't easy to sell when you are not feeling too fit, but too often a slight cold becomes in the mind influenza. A touch of back-ache becomes in the mind a slipped disc . . . This mental attitude keeps the salesman at home.

Bob Robinson had had a colostomy operation, with all the problems that that entails in the aftermath. Yet I never remember him taking a day off from selling. On one occasion, when I attempted to sympathise with him and praise him for his dedication – he was, by then, a field manager – he replied, 'If I were to start giving in to pain and discomfort I'd keep on giving in. I keep telling my salesmen that they mustn't give way easily; it's so easy for a salesman to stay at home because, unlike working at head office, it need hardly be noticed'.

By this time I think you will be getting ready to disagree with me, but all I am giving you are facts, and reasons why some men reach the top while others complain that they have never had the opportunity. I am not judging people, I am only repeating what happened in the past and what others have told me: And you must admit that Robinson had the right mental attitude.

Charlie Briars was a short, stocky, tough Brummy. He exemplified the RMA story of the salesmen sent to a Pacific island to sell shoes. The story is an old one but you may not have heard it.

The first salesman reported back quickly, 'Returning home – the natives here don't wear shoes'.

The second salesman, with the right mental attitude, reported, 'I shall be here for months. Tremendous opportunities – the natives here don't wear shoes. But they will!' That was Briar's attitude when he took over the Birmingham/Coventry territory. His predecessor nad asked to be moved to another territory 'because', he insisted, 'the factories here are all dominated by the car industry, with working areas far too large for our small units'. (Remember, this was before our days of full air-conditioning.)

An early report from Briars read: 'Wonderful opportunities here! Austins' have so many small sections in their big shops which need the special treatment our units can give'.

So remember, when told by other salesmen that 'The area is saturated', 'They only buy on price here', 'You don't stand a chance with the supermarket chains these days, it's all central buying', 'Don't cold call there, you'll never get an interview', just smile, and ignore the advice.

Chris Heyworth, one of the truly *greats* who worked for us, achieved outstanding success, as a salesman, as an area manager, and as a field sales manager. He put into practice all the many aspects of human relations which have now become standard teaching in business schools and training organisations, and are included in all books and magazines on salesmanship.

He claimed that he built a wonderful team of salesmen because they were all so good and tried so hard, but in fact he built the team spirit because he applied human relations every day of his life. He taught his salesmen how to make the buyers their friends.

I suppose Uncle Joe would have listed most aspects of human relations as 'the way to sell yourself'. When I asked his advice in the early days, he would often reply, 'Before you can sell a product you have first to sell yourself'.

It sounds horrible these days, doesn't it? But it was a standard expression when I began selling. The phrase *to sell yourself* seems to imply degradation of oneself in order to achieve one's ends. It was nothing of the kind! It meant then, as it means now, simply acting in a manner towards others which will enhance their respect for you. A bit of a mouthful, but it is a fact that we only buy from people we dislike if we have to – if there is no other choice. And very rarely does that happen. Most buyers do have a choice, and when all things are equal, and even when they are not quite so equal, they prefer to buy from someone they like and trust.

In a survey carried out by our research division on *Buyers' Likes and Dislikes of Salesmen*, regardless of the product or service offered, the dislikes included those who tell funny stories, have body odours, talk too much, exaggerate, have an untidy appearance; while likes included integrity, knowing the product and keeping promises. When invited to make comments, 94 per cent of the respondents used words to this effect: 'We buy from the salesmen we like and trust most'.

We learn from experience, as well as by research, what motivates people, but the tenets of human relations came naturally to Chris Heyworth.

He was known as Uncle Chris both by his salesmen and many of his customers. How that came about I do not know; it just happened. Suddenly we were all calling him Uncle Chris, as a term of our regard and affection.

You cannot switch the main tenets of human relations on and off. They have to become a part of your character and personality, which will spill over into your private life from selling – or the other way around.

The two main features of human relations which can make such a difference to your success, to your life generally, to your relationship with customers and your company, are *Do not criticise* and *Give praise when praise is due*.

Avoid unnecessary criticism

We are all apt to criticise too much and give praise too seldom. Yet praise is the greatest motivator of all when it is deserved, and criticism can be the greatest demotivator.

Think about yourself for a moment. When you show a friend your new car, a newly plucked rose from your garden, or a holiday brochure depicting the hotel you stayed at when you were in Sardinia, you don't want to hear, 'I do wish you had asked my advice! This car has a rust problem', 'A friend of mine had one of these, and he had awful trouble after that snowy winter' or 'You should have bought an XYZ.' Nor do you want a friend looking at the rose to complain, 'You've given this too much fertiliser, the petals are misshapen', or looking at your holiday brochure to scoff, 'Sardinia! Whatever made you think of going there? That's where they kidnap people!'

Does such unnecessary criticism please or upset you? I bet it's the latter. You want praise for your rose. You want someone to tell you how delightful the hotel in Sardinia looks. But most of all you want the bonnet of the car to be patted, and someone to say, 'I've heard it's very good!'

Of course there are times before an action has been taken when advice that could be considered criticism can, and should, be given. There are other times when mistakes are made, when changes have to be effected, and some form of criticism is necessary. Such criticism is, however, always easier to accept if it is diluted with some praise.

Back to the rose again. You wouldn't object to this: 'You know, John, I've always looked on you as a very good gardener, but from your experience, don't you think. . .?'; or 'You wouldn't get a better car for your purpose, but I'll tell you what I did with my last car. I had the underneath rustproofed. It's well worth while, you know'.

Ask yourself this question: *What happens when your sales manager or director, your spouse, or members of the same team praise your efforts?* You may appear to act a little diffidently, but inside aren't you glowing with pleasure, and aren't you motivated to try that little bit harder next time?

At one of our courses Uncle Chris gave two examples of how direct or indirect criticism can lose customers. The first occurred when he was calling with a salesman on a small restaurant. The objective was to sell a fan-ozoniser, intended mainly to deodorise the air.

The salesman's approach was, 'I should like to tell you how we can definitely kill all the smells in your restaurant. . .' He had moved away from the standard approach and was trying to impress his supervisor with the originality of his thinking.

'We have no smells here', replied the Italian restaurant owner, scowling his annoyance. Why should he have been annoyed? Most restaurants smell of cooking odours, some worse than others, and this was one of the worst. But it was the implied criticism that the restaurant smelled that was so wrong. Smell? Ugh!

The salesman should have said, 'Your customers can now enjoy eating out of door meals indoors. Our ozonisers generate fresh, odour-free air which means that in your restaurant. . .' Uncle Chris said, 'Nothing he could say afterwards could put matters right, and they made no headway'.

The second example was when calling with a salesman on a furniture store. The salesman, having learned that praise is always acceptable, said, 'What a nice little place you have here!' True, it was small, but the owner believed that he owned a furniture emporium. He didn't think it was small, and he was hurt at the implied criticism that he was the owner of a little shop.

Once a prospective buyer is upset, it is very difficult to put things right. Objections can be overcome, stalling excuses can be defeated but hurt someone's feelings and it can be a long time before things can be put right, if they ever can be.

Think about it. Think about it again, and then make

up your mind that you will always refrain from criticism; and even when that criticism is essential, just think
twice before voicing it. But whenever you see anything
worthy of praise, at home, in the office, in a factory or
shop, then give it, and give it lavishly.

Here is one more example which covers the industrial field, and which is given because otherwise, readers
in this field of activity may believe that the lesson
doesn't apply to them.

Bert Perkins, once a director of Herberts, then the
largest machine-tool manufacturers in Europe, tells of
being asked by a customer for his opinion of a new
machine which the customer had just purchased from
Germany – one not in direct competition with Herberts' range. Perkins thought he was being completely
honest and helpful when he criticised many aspects of
the new machine. But did it please the customer who
had asked for an honest opinion? Not at all! Perkins
never got another order from that customer.

He told me subsequently, 'Never, never criticise if an
action has been taken, a purchase made, a decision
arrived at. To do so will only result in antagonising
someone and creating ill-feeling. If no action has been
taken, then it's a different matter – but one should still
not criticise then, only give advice'.

Another example of human relations in action is
typified by Fred Boyes. He believed in loyalty – a word
to make the cynics shudder.

Fred would often say to his team, 'If you can't be
loyal, get out'. A bit stark, and possibly difficult to
apply for many people, but not for salesmen.

It's hard to speak well of your company if you believe
you have been treated unfairly, yet you can't leave the
job because jobs are scarce – but this doesn't apply to
selling, because good salesmen can always obtain other
jobs, and if a salesman therefore cannot be loyal, he
should look elsewhere for a living. Loyalty has many

meanings, but to the salesman it means not belittling his company to others.

For example, many a salesman has said such things as, 'I agree with you, our service is dreadful, and I agree that you can't get Bill Thomson between twelve and three, he's always out to lunch at that time'; or, to a new recruit, 'Don't take any notice of what they taught you at the training school – it's armchair stuff, that's all. You listen to me...'; or, to a fellow salesman, 'Everyone inflates expenses. Old Pinhead in Accounts is too old and doesn't notice a thing'.

Loyalty doesn't mean remaining with a company for ever, or not criticising anyone at head office – giving them a good blasting, when talking over problems with close relatives. It does mean standing up for your company, right or wrong, when you are with customers, and not undermining the morale of colleagues because you are upset and simply want to let off steam or pass on gossip.

Keep it tidy

Too many salesmen have the wrong mental attitude towards their sales kits, demonstration units, cars...

One of our other managers was John Cosburn, known as Tidy Cosburn. On every occasion he met a salesman he would check that salesman's kit, samples, literature, and car. He was quite tough with them. His salesmen may have got a little tired of his continual lecturing, but they responded. His team learned the right mental attitude by good teaching from their supervisor.

Why not have a look at your sales kit now? Is there any dog-eared literature, out of date material, any lack of general cleanliness? At our courses we have a notice above the platform reading: *Does this apply to me?* This is the message we want every delegate to have imprinted on his mind. Too often they believe that indirect criticism applies to the person in the next seat, but not to themselves. So here is another aspect of the right mental attitude:

Always condition your mind to reflect continually on the advice given at our courses – DOES IT APPLY TO ME?

To switch from the subject for a moment to those of you who believe our fate is predestined, Cosburn's was decided when he emigrated to Australia. It was during the time of the Cuban crisis and Cosburn believed that there would be an atomic war, and that he should not risk the lives of his wife and children in this country. Six months after arriving in Australia, he was killed in a road accident.

RMA and up-and-downers

In every salesforce there is an up-and-downer, or a yo-yo salesman, as they are sometimes called. When he is up, taking orders and being praised, he is very up and is sometimes difficult to handle, because of his constant demands. When he hits a sticky patch, he is so down he can't see good in anything or anyone. The territory is wrong, the product is wrong, his sales manager is wrong, even the weather is wrong, and he mainly blames his lack of success on lack of help from head office.

In sport, in the theatre, as well as in selling, there is a stream of up-and-downers; but an actor will still act to the best of his ability, even when he is very down. A yo-yo salesman, however, loses most of his selling skills when things go wrong.

Unfortunately he is incurable – well, I suppose he could cure himself, otherwise I shouldn't be writing

about him. No pep talk can help. Only after reading
this section of the book and saying to himself, '*Does it
apply to me*?' can he help to alleviate his sufferings
when down and ensure a little more commonsense
when up.

That is the wrong mental attitude. It is bad for the
salesman, but it is a complete disaster for the manager.

Exercise stretch

Have you the right mental attitude towards achieving
your target?

George Drexler, the dynamic managing director who
built up the Ofrex Group, once said to me, 'What
annoys me is when a salesman, on being asked how he
is faring, replies, 'I get my share of the market'.

It's the same when a manager says to me, when I am
about to travel overseas, 'Don't worry – I'll hold the
fort for you'.

A share of the market is not good enough for me,
and neither are fort-holders. A salesman should never
be satisfied with his 'share of the market'. He wants to
eat into a competitor's share and get more of a share for
himself, because of his skills and his drive. I want
managers, when I am away, to make decisions, take
actions to increase my business – not just to be happy
to 'hold everything' until I return.'

Drexler is right! Exercise *Stretch* will prove the
justification of his remarks. It entails your company
introducing an incentive which rewards very highly the
achievements well above target – some might say, the
almost impossible dream, but no high quality salesman
would ever turn away from such a challenge. He will
stretch himself, and will discover that by greater concentration on time-management practices, by constantly
reminding himself of the basic concepts and skills of

salesmanship, he will achieve targets that he never believed possible.

We have proved this over and over again in our own organisation, and the many companies our consultants have advised. But even the greatest of salesmen rarely works to more than 60 per cent of his capacity. Salespeople will always pull out their best when negotiating for a big deal, but overlook the high turnover which can be achieved by giving everyone a chance to buy. They have the mentality of the star Test cricketer, who does well in Test matches but in a country ground, watched by three men, two dogs and a couple of children, finds it hard to play to his full potential. The great men in sport never feel like that; they always give of their best – and so does the star salesman.

Donald Reid was another truly great salesman, who did so much to help our company. Now pause for a shock: he joined us at the age of sixty-five to sell our air-conditioning units. Previously, he had been a professional singer, appearing once at a Royal Command Performance at the Palladium. He retired at the age of eighty-two.

How about that for those who say we're too old at forty!

At the time of writing this book, Donald and his beloved Margaret live in the South of Spain, enjoying a well-earned retirement, achieved by his own efforts.

Here's another surprise for you: he would never work for a salary, and he was offered quite a good one. To put him on a high salary would have been to our benefit, although that was not our consideration when we made the offer. We thought he would like the security, but we never attempted to persuade him away from straight commission.

He certainly had the right mental attitude to win us all over to being on his side at all times, and to make us want to stand by him, whatever happened. He would never take a penny in expenses from us.

'How silly!' 'How ridiculous!' I can hear you saying. But I'm only telling you the facts. His right mental attitude did, I am sure, help towards his promotion, and helped us to ensure that he would have no financial worries in the future.

As a member of the Variety Artists' Club, every year he invited to their annual dinner some of his customers, and also my brother and me. His customers thought as highly of him as we did – affection would be the better term. But the lesson to be learned from Donald's success was that it is easier to sell to the chief executive of any company than to the managers. He proved that with the right mental attitude an appointment with the chairman or managing director was not difficult to obtain. The wrong mental attitude is, 'But they won't see me'. They will!

He was one of the first to recognise the potential of *conversational selling*, which really means that irrespective of the standing of the buyer, managing director, general manager ... talk to him as you would to a friend or relation. Donald said so many times, 'You can only succeed with the Top Brass when they believe you are their equal – *conversational selling* can achieve that end, whether by telephone or at a personal call'.

Difficult? Not really! Donald did it – and so have many other salesmen. *Conversational selling* will be covered in a later chapter.

Donald was a quality salesman, and there is no mission impossible to the quality salesman.

Donald, we are still in your debt!

A salesman wears many hats

A salesman with the right mental attitude will in his time play many parts. At every call his main endeavour is to discover needs – to explain benefits – and to turn those needs into wants. This will always take up some 60 per cent or more of a call, but during that call he may have to put on different hats.

1　The ambassador

The ambassador in a foreign country has to persuade the local ministers that steps taken by his own government are right and proper. If there are differences of opinion between countries, he has to iron them out, while never giving the slightest indication that his country is in the wrong.

Every salesman at some time or another has to wear the hat of an ambassador. This means that he must be tactful at all times, even-tempered when his company has been criticised, and able to defend it in a manner which will not antagonise the buyer. Like ambassadors, the salesman must be diplomatic, so that when carrying out his company's instructions, the buyer will almost believe that the salesman is conferring a favour upon him. This applies particularly when discussing credit terms, special discounts, or problems over service. A foreign ambassador must uphold the dignity and honour of his country in all circumstances – and so must the salesman, so far as his company is concerned.

2　The negotiator

The hallmark of a negotiator is that he must leave the buyer with the impression that he – the buyer – has had his requests met, when in reality there has been a compromise over each one of them. Negotiating is an art which must be learned by the salesman and is essential when, after the presentation has been completed and the decision almost arrived at, the buyer wants to negotiate different terms or technical changes.

3 *The public-relations officer*

The salesman must be able to create a complete awareness on the part of the buyer of every aspect of his company's activities.

When we read an article in a newspaper which gives information about a company, to the benefit of that company, few people are aware that it is the work of a public relations officer.

A salesman should also, during many a visit, draw a buyer's attention to some achievement on the part of his company which, although only of passing interest to the buyer, may still have an effect on the outcome of the visit, or simply increase the buyer's confidence in the company. For example, he should mention a special award to any member of the staff, obviously the Queen's Award, if that has been granted, overseas successes, export successes, etc. The PR's job is to sell, indirectly, by giving information which may lead to a greater awareness of a company's successes.

4 *The advocate*

Like the lawyer in court, the salesman has to be able to marshal his facts and remember them. He must be able to build his case so strongly that the judge – in this case the buyer – will sum up in his favour.

A salesman must be a good advocate.

5 *A management/marketing consultant*

A salesman is often called a problem-solver, and it is true that on many a call he has to help solve a problem for the benefit of the buyer and his own company. He also has to discover a buyer's real needs, and advise how those needs can be fulfilled.

6 A planner

No managing director can succeed if he cannot make plans in advance to lead to the greater success of his company. No salesman can succeed unless he is able to plan ahead, so that he knows exactly what he has to do when facing a customer, or when he is about to call on a customer.

7 An Economist

I have heard many an extravagant salesman say, 'I never cut my costs – I go out to earn more to meet my commitments'.

Big talk! Wrong thinking! Obviously a salesman must fight hard to achieve ever increasing turnover, but too many salesmen are big spenders. They buy houses, perhaps too large for their requirements, with the consequence that they suffer crippling mortgages. They buy that extra car, and never say 'No' to any domestic appliance request. When the expenditure becomes greater than the income, in spite of striving hard to increase sales, the increased earnings may not result in ends being met. Then what happens? The salesman blames his company for his misfortunes. He seeks an increase in salary when there is no justification for it. He begins reading advertising columns, convincing himself that somewhere, some place, there is a more highly paid job – one more commensurate with his ability.

The right mental attitude is for him to learn more about finance, from the viewpoint of his company, his customers, and his own family. He needs to learn about cash flow, budgeting, forecasting, the real meaning of profits, why it is financially beneficial for his customer to buy his products, why his company must sometimes make decisions based solely on financial requirements.

Once a week a salesman should put on his financial hat, to consider the decisions to be made from an economic viewpoint. A salesman who worries about meeting additional bills will find it extremely difficult, if not impossible, to increase his turnover to help meet those bills. A worried salesman can never sell to his full potential. The right menal attitude, which will enable him to study the many implications of finance, will help solve problems.

8   A researcher

Ask any sales executive how he rates salesmen's research and the answer will probably be: 'Too slanted! Not objective, and often dependent on how a salesman feels on a particular day'. Salesmen tend to prove what they want to prove, but they should be ideal researchers. However, they can only act in an objective, or at least a semi-objective, manner if they have had training in research.

Far too few companies give training in how to research, but the salesman with the right mental attitude will take it upon himself to research continually – not to find fault with everyone at head office, not to prove what he is always claiming, that delivery is impossible and credit collections upset his best customers, but to provide himself with factual information which will help him to satisfy customer needs.

Think not of what your company can do for you, but of what you can do for your company.

9   The managing director

The salesman is the managing director and sole shareholder of his own company. He has to make decisions on which his future might depend, he has to motivate himself, and discipline himself. He must decide on the allocation of time for study, for researching, for planning, for telephoning, for report-writing... Like all managing directors, he must use time-management. As his own managing director he must be demanding but fair – he must not readily accept excuses, but should set himself high targets and drive himself hard for his family, himself, and his company.

Not a compliment

Selling should be an unobtrusive art; it is sometimes termed 'the gentle art of giving other people your own way'. That is why the star salesmen depicted on screen are so untrue to life.

When a good salesman sells, the buyer is unaware that he has been persuaded to take action which he would have preferred to defer. Why defer? Because nearly all buyers prefer to do so unless they have to replenish stocks, etc. That is why a salesman uses honest persuasion to convince a buyer that it is to his – the buyer's – benefit to place an order for his services or products.

When the star salesman is at work, the buyer believes that he is not being persuaded in any way. He believes that he is making decisions without being influenced by the salesman.

Now for the other side of the picture. When a salesman says to me with great pride, 'Reg Banks – you know him, he's the buyer at ABC – said to me this morning, "You are the best salesman I've met for weeks!" ', I tell him, as kindly as possible, that he should not be so pleased with himself because he has failed, he has given the game away, he has been seen through, he has been downgraded... The buyer is not being complimentary, he is putting the salesman in his place.

If ever that happens to you in the future, be objective. Realise that in some way you have acted like a 'typical salesman' of the screen. Decide to change, and sell in a conversational manner. Better be an unrecognised great salesman than one who makes a buyer annoyed at being treated as someone unable to make a decision without being prompted.

The star salesman makes the buyer happy with himself – happy that he has made a decision.

That is good selling!

RMA

The right mental attitude is of such great benefit to all who sell, yet it is so hard to discipline oneself to change attitudes, and think positively. Take a deep breath. Here are twelve more aspects of salesmanship which can be included under the heading of RMA:

1 Always be courteous

You always are? Wait a moment – how often have you been treated discourteously by salespeople in shops? At least once, surely! So check on yourself, in case you are the 'once' to the other person.

2 Good manners

We always believe our manners are perfect, but then we are all so good at self-deception.

One question: would you smoke a cigarette yourself after offering one to the customer and receiving a negative response, to which you then say, 'Do you mind if I do?' That has happened to me several times when I have been the buyer. I usually say that I do mind, but others, more kindly, may give their approval

while still feeling most annoyed. And the buyer who is
annoyed does not buy!

3   Apologise

Do you quickly say 'I'm sorry' if you are in the wrong,
or even only slightly in the wrong? Two little words
which can win over so many irate customers!

4   Admit your mistakes

Never attempt to cover up. By admitting your mistakes
you will be an unusual person, but one who will be
respected by others.

5   Don't gossip

Avoid tittle-tattle talk with customers about other
customers, competitors, your own colleagues at head
office. . .

6   Have a nice day!

We're all a little tired of being told to have a nice day,
but to say 'Thank you' is something which is always
welcome. Thank a customer for his orders, but, most of
all, always remember to thank the buyer's assistants for
any help received.

7   Importance

As you know, we all like to feel important – managing
directors, buyers, and, most of all, assistants. Never
convey the impression that the customer's job is not
highly important, and all those who work under him
also have important work to do.

8 Time-wasting

Don't tell funny stories. Don't waste customers' time by talking about your family, your holidays, gardening... But always be willing to listen to his or her stories about their families, their holidays, or their gardens. Listen intently; don't be a pouncer or try to cap their stories. Don't interrupt. Let others do the talking, and you do most of the listening.

9 Proximity

Never stand too close to a buyer. Always keep your distance.

10 I don't know

Simply say, 'I don't know' if you are not sure of an answer to a customer's question. To say, 'I don't know' is forgivable. To try to brazen it out is unforgivable.

11 Be cheerful

However you feel, however depressing are the newspaper headlines, however short you are of cash, you must still be cheerful when confronting a buyer. No one likes to do business with a perpetual moaner. Let the buyer moan if he wants to – but don't respond in kind.

12 Mannerisms

Do we irritate others with our mannerisms? Buyers emphasise that mannerisms can cause loss of concentration and may even result in an interview being cut short. Beware of mannerisms such as looking anywhere except at the buyer. He feels you are looking at some object above his head. Watch for the repetition

of words or clichés – 'OK', 'sort of', 'by and large', 'in
this day and age', etc. Don't hold a handkerchief in
your hand, or drum with your fingertips on the arm of a
chair, desk, or table.

Check on your mannerisms. Better still, ask a friend
– a good friend – to tell you about them.

Your first test

The principles of RMA have been tried and tested, not
only within our own group, not only within our own
industrial companies, but also worldwide. Keep to
these principles, day after day, week after week, month
after month. Check regularly with this chapter to make
sure that you are keeping to the fundamentals of RMA.
Do that, and you will not only prove that you have the
right mental attitude, but you will be setting a very firm
foundation for your future success.

4 Buyer motivation

Before we can analyse our service, product, our company, to discover every conceivable benefit to build into our offer to our customers or potential customers, we must, first, analyse the reasons why buyers buy. Only after we have pinpointed these motivators can we ally specific motivators to the needs of the buyer. Everything will then fall neatly into place.

At times we all buy, at times we all sell. When we buy, we act no differently from our customers, to whom we sell our old car, garden mower, or house. We become salesmen even if we are bankers, farm workers, or waiters. When a house is up for sale, and those awful people who only want to look round call, the householder is in a selling situation and will react accordingly, using many of a salesman's techniques: for example, a fear motivator, saying, 'We had a couple in this morning who were very interested. They are telephoning this afternoon'. If the prospective buyers are interested, or even semi-interested, they may be fearful of losing what now becomes a most wanted house.

Alternatively, the householder might say, 'Another good point is that there isn't any ground for the Council to build houses around here'. That may not be a very moral stand, but all the householder means is that anyone buying his house will not find that changes in the area will lower the value of the property. They may in fact raise its price – a profit motivator.

Then there's the householder who says, 'It's been such a happy house for us, full of laughter and fun as the children grew up. But now, we need something smaller'. That householder is using a sentimental motivator to appeal to the buyer's yearning for a peaceful house to live in.

I've also heard this one: 'It's a part of the Duchy of Whatsit's land, you know'. Why mention that? To satisfy the pride of the purchaser, pride at living so near the aristocracy of the country. Some may not feel that way, but quite a few do!

In addition, of course, there's the householder's plea that the house should be bought because 'it's not like those Jerry-built affairs' – the implication being that the house is as solid as a rock and will last for generations. That will satisfy the buyer's need for caution, or self-preservation.

The reason I am making this point is that if ever you are in this situation, you will consider all the motivators before the buyers start to call. That is what we are going to do now, in a general sense.

Those who want to buy a house will usually have a main motive and a subsidiary motive. The main motive might be that a doctor wants to live near his practice; a subsidiary motive the need for extra bathrooms or additional living space.

Nearly always, when we make a purchase, there is a main and a subsidiary reason. If, for example, we buy a tie, we may believe that we are buying it to match a particular suit or shirt, or to replace a frayed neckpiece. But another reason may well be the pleasure it gives to someone else – a girl friend, or wife.

If the salesman in the shop is aware of any subsidiary motivation, he may mention how much the tie will be approved by others, and that could close the sale for him. In the same way managers and professional buyers are motivated by thoughts of pleasing their chief or directors.

We buy a golf club because of the pleasure we think it will give us, and pleasure is a powerful motivator. A subsidiary reason may be a technical feature, which the golfer may have read in some magazine or other will help him with his swing.

When a managing director agrees to his photograph being used in an advertisement, he may believe that he is reluctantly agreeing to the advertising agents' advice purely for the sake of the company or to benefit company policy. He is misleading himself. The real reason is that it makes him feel just a little more important – that his family and friends will realise the important position he holds. It will boost his image, since many of his friends do not realise what a good job he has. So to make others feel important is also a motivator. It may be a subsidiary motivator, but it is one, nevertheless.

Now let me tell you about another motivator, by explaining my worst ever sale. I was calling on the owner of a small newsagent's and tobacconist's with the object of selling him a small vending machine. Being honest, I insisted that he would get good results from a two-column unit, but he showed little interest.

I had almost given up when he picked up a brochure I had placed on the counter, looked through it, and while I continued to insist that he only required a small unit, he pointed to the largest one, a massive twelve-column double decker, almost the size of his shop window.

'That's the one I like', he said.

I said, 'You don't need that here'.

Can you imagine saying 'No' to such a request?

Well, I did! And to make matters worse, he had to insist on buying the larger machine before I gave way. Then he paid in cash. I had felt sorry for him, believing that he could afford no more than our smallest unit.

There were several lessons I learned that day. The first was never to judge a prospect by his clothes, the size of his office or factory, or the position of his shop. In this case the newsagent was quite a wealthy person, owning a lot of property nearby.

The next lesson I learned was that envy is also a motivator. A friend of that newsagent had a similar shop some way away, and he had recently installed one of a competitor's large double-decker units. The competitor was for ever boasting about having the largest unit in the area, and of being congratulated by his customers on his enterprise. Although my newsagent was obviously buying to make an additional profit, his secondary motivator – and a very strong one – was envy of a competitor. If I had been more skilled at that time, I should first have discussed needs, and would have discovered that, small as the shop was, it was in an excellent position and highly profitable. Therefore the larger unit in itself could still have been the right one for that particular newsagent, even if I had not introduced the secondary motivator of how others would react to his enterprise – especially his competitor.

Underlying motives in buying

One salesman may have a price advantage, another an efficiency advantage, a third special promotions, another excellent packaging... But each may lose orders by thinking in terms of motivating a buyer because of one particular advantage.

The salesman's objective must always be to include in his sales offer all the motivational forces which will impel the buyer to buy. It is often the secondary motivator which will turn the tide in his favour.

The rational and the emotional

On most occasions when we buy, we act rationally; but on others we are motivated solely by emotion – flowers for the one we love, an extravagant purchase for a child. Pride, we know, is another emotional reason.

Often sentiment plays a part in our decision. There was a Buy British campaign which implied that even if British prices were slightly higher, for sentimental reasons alone we should buy British.

Sometimes we buy from companies well-known to us – father, son, and so on – when a competitor may have a slight edge over such family concerns. When a salesman says, 'We are local and we can give you immediate service', he is using a *satisfaction of caution* as the main motivator, as well as *sentiment*.

One of the strongest of all emotional appeals is the approval of others, which we touched on before. Every buyer likes that pat on the back:

'You have bought well!'

'What an excellent window display!'

'How wise of you to change to leasing'. . .

Every salesman is aware therefore, when completing his offer analysis, that he must discover ways and means of appealing to the emotional section of the mind of the buyer, as well as to the rational. The emotional stems from a lower part of the brain, yet continually a higher order of mental reasoning gives way to a lower order of emotional response. Over and over again history shows that emotions have taken precedence over rational thinking.

Classification of buying motives

Rational	Emotional
Gain, or saving money	Satisfaction of pride
Satisfaction of caution	Pleasure
Benefit to health	Sentimental reasons
Protection and security	Fear

Utility value	Envy Approval of others Social achievements To feel important

A more specific classification of rational motives applicable to most salesmen is:

Profit	Direct gain of money – return from investment – cost reduction – increased output – less absenteeism – quicker selling lines
Efficiency	Performance – it is faster – easier to handle – less risk of breakdown – less complicated – more powerful – quieter in operation – works to finer limits
Protection and security	Confidence in supplier – guaranteed standards – guaranteed deliveries – eliminating risk to employees – good after-sales service – wards off competition – heavily backed by advertising
Appearance	Good design – compact – modern in concept – wide colour range – appealing packaging
Durability	Long life – less maintenance – withstands rough usage – less risk of breakdown – customer satisfaction
Utility	Saving in time – labour – effort – more convenient to use – easier to handle

Health	Better working conditions – reduces strain – better environment – benefit to employees (canteen, food, air-conditioning, lighting, etc.,) – health – value to customers

Because of their understanding of buyers' motivation, salespeople are able to build a strong sales offer – one which will appeal to the widest range of buyers. All salesmen must remind themselves that a prime motivator is helping a buyer to solve problems.

Creating a 'Want'

No company, however large, can afford to buy everything offered to it – more luxurious offices, a head office in the centre of town, private executive aircraft, a larger canteen, more sophisticated computers, bigger cars for salesmen, an exhibition coach. In addition, no managing director can agree to all the demands made upon him by the various departments in his organisation. A managing director has to withstand this type of pressure continually: research and development want new testing equipment, the works manager cannot do without new paint-spraying booths, the production manager must have that computerised machine, the transport manager requests more lorries, while the warehouse manager wants extra space to house larger stocks.

To add to the list, the PRO conscious of the company image wants goodwill advertising, the financial director wants different computers, the cleaners want new brooms, and the canteen manager more cutlery. The salesman therefore has to compete for a firm's cash. He has to make that managing director or buyer give his product or service priority over requests for computers, paint-spraying booths, cutlery etc. How then can a salesman use his knowledge of motivators to persuade a buyer to give his product or service priority?

The answer is *by creating a very special want* in the mind of the buyer.

There are specific areas in which a salesman can create the right atmosphere for a buyer to *want* the merchandise, products, or services he is offering. Even a specifying authority – architect, consulting engineer, welfare officer – will only make a decision when he or she *wants* to favour one supplier instead of another.

Understanding motivational forces allows a salesman to create a desire to buy by appealing to a buyer's *wants*. What we all *want* when we buy are benefits for ourselves, our families, or our company; and if we are retailers, then we want benefits for our customers. There is no one point in a sale when desire is created, any more than there is one time only when confidence is established. A salesman is always building confidence in himself and his company, and every time he shows a buyer a benefit, he should be creating a *want*. The salesman who builds benefit after benefit is the professional who gets more than his share of the business.

Understanding motivational forces allows a salesman to concentrate on the main benefits which appeal to a particular buyer. Let us say that:

Buyer A is mainly motivated by *profitability*.
Buyer B is mainly motivated by *security*.
Buyer C is mainly motivated by *efficiency*.

Salesman Lenton will show Buyer A the benefit of profitability to be derived from his product or service, and will bring up those benefits (quick turnover, high demand) again and again. Salesman Goodhew, selling to B, will concentrate on proving the benefits of regular deliveries, 24-hour service and maintenance of standards. Salesman Owen, selling to Buyer C, demonstrates that the efficiency of his product must benefit the buyer's production line. The professional salesman, while concentrating on the main benefits offered by his product or service will, however, never overlook all the subsidiary benefits which may finally motivate a buyer to buy.

Salesmen also create *wants* by talking in terms of what a product *does* rather than what it *is*.

Do you buy a mattress because a salesman tells you that there is a cushioning of fleece on one side of the mattress and white cotton felt on the other? Or do you buy because the professional salesman has told you that you will feel extra warm with this mattress in the winter, and cool in the summer?

Does a buyer buy because the salesman, steeped in technicalities says, 'This melamine–formaldehyde resin, when used in a mixture with alkyd resins, gives a much faster heat cure than when a ureaformaldehyde resin alone is used. The outstanding characteristics which urea resins supply to films are further enhanced with melamine resins, which are then resistant to various chemical reagents and maintain durability and colour retention to heat and light'? Or does he buy because the professional salesman has said, 'The melamine–formaldehyde resin is used with alkyd resins so that you will be able to produce a porcelain-like appearance, resistant to abrasions and heat'?

Does a buyer buy because a salesman says, 'Our new pack is made of double strength *Riebelene* and to open it you have only to press a small plastic button'? Or does he buy because the salesman says, '*Your* customers will keep coming back for more, because the *Riebelene* pack means a negligible risk of spillage – no more mopping up – and housewives will no longer ruin their nails trying to open the pack'?

Buyers buy for the latter reasons – those given by
the professional salesmen who always translate technicalities into direct benefits to the buyer or his company. Elmer Wheeler summed it up years ago when he
coined the phrase, '*Don't sell the steak – sell the
sizzle!*'

Motivation by filling needs and stimulating wants

In every industry there are basic needs catered for by a
host of suppliers – raw materials, component parts,
standard tools, packaging supplies, and every kind of
merchandise, consumer goods, and consumer durables.
These needs can be counted by the hundreds in some
factories, thousands in others, and by dozens in shops
and stores. Suppliers of basic needs usually operate in a
highly competitive market. Every week a buyer will see
salesmen eager to tell him why he should buy, from
them instead of from his current suppliers, disinfec-
tants, ballbearings, cleaning materials, switchgear,
overalls for staff, electric motors, soaps, detergents,
dresses, coats. . .

What motivates a buyer to change suppliers, or agree
to a change in the specification of the product he is
buying regularly from one of his suppliers? He will only
change his mind if there are likely to be additional
benefits from switching to a new supplier, or agreeing
to any changes in specification.

To change the mind of a buyer, a salesman must
therefore turn his basic need into a *want* – a *want* for
the salesman's product or service. As the main buying
benefit is usually already obtainable from the present
supplier, the salesman who is competing to fill a basic
need must be sure of selling every subsidiary benefit
offered by his product, because one of these could be
the motivator to change that basic need into a *want* for
his product.

Unrecognised or real needs

An *unrecognised need*, usually referred to as the *real need*, is sometimes obvious, sometimes not. For example, before domestic refrigerators came on the market, although block ice was often used to keep food cool, in most households food was kept in cellars or food safes, or was stood in bowls of water. So far as the people in those days were concerned, their need was being filled. The food was just that shade cooler, lasted just that short time longer than if it were left in an outside warmer atmosphere, so that these simple methods filled the need. Eventually, when household refrigerators were marketed, filling the *real need*, there was a great deal of resistance to buying. Housewives believed that, except perhaps in very hot weather, they had no food deterioration problems, and they were content with their food safes, etc. Salesmen who sold refrigerators in those days had a very difficult job persuading people to *want* a refrigerator, because the housewives did not recognise that *real need*.

But recognition of *real needs* is not confined to the householder. Skilled buyers, brilliant managing directors, heads of production units often do not recognise their *real needs*. A managing director may believe that his *basic need* is satisfied by an outsize card-index filing system, a system which has grown over the years, entailing the use of many filing cabinets and causing overcrowding in offices.

'We'll have to move', says the officer manager.

'Yes', agrees the managing director, 'I think it's coming to that.'

But his *real need* could be for a micro-film system installation. Such an installation would save a great deal of space, and retrieval, taking only seconds, would enable staff who are constantly having to search the files for information to be better employed. The filing cabinets could be disposed of, and there would be an improved service both to customers and salesmen. The *need* being unrecognised, a salesman selling micro-film systems would have to emphasise these and other benefits until the *want* was created.

Often in the retail trade there is an unrecognised need for better quality and higher-priced products, but the retailer is obsessed with the belief that in his district no one will pay the higher price of the quality goods. Retailers and wholesalers often have to be persuaded that they do not need more of X, costing £1, but should stock Y, at a cost of £1+, and create new business for themselves.

Here is an example from Nu-Aire Ltd. a company within our own group, which saw that a whole dimension in building design could be opened up, if a certain product were made available. The building industry did not at first recognise that *need*.

British building regulations state that a toilet/bathroom must be provided either with a window which can be opened or with a mechanical extractor system which changes the air in the room a specified number of times in the hour. In addition, various local recommendations specify that the fan system serving these internal rooms must be of the standby type, so that should the fan fail, the reserve fan automatically takes over. All these rules are designed to protect the health of tenants and are strictly enforced by both the public health inspector and the building inspectorate.

Until about 1967 the need for ventilation had been met by special fans designed to serve internal bathrooms and WCs. They were limited to sizes suitable for a number of rooms linked together by a common duct system, and therefore the only occasions on which internal bathrooms and WCs were used were in fairly high rise buildings. Because of this, low and medium-rise buildings were not designed with internal bathrooms and WCs. On the other hand, there were quite obvious pressures on the building industry to bring these rooms into the internal core of the construction. The reasons were:

1 Lack of suitable building land and its cost made narrow frontage dwellings attractive to the developers and architects.
2 The grouping together of all services in the central core reduced costs.

Nu-Aire Ltd rcognised a *need* and designed a range of self-regulating small units suitable for ventilating individual internal bathrooms and WCs. The units satisfied the various standards, were inexpensive, and, most important, they could be selected and detailed by the architect without help from specialised service engineers.

After the *real need* was explained by Nu-Aire salesmen, the demand was created. These units subsequently directly influenced architecture in Britain, so that today internal bathroom/WCs are a feature of dwellings, from low to high rise types; but in spite of the fact that these units were unique, Nu-Aire salesmen had, time and time again, to make the *need* for the units recognised, and then *create the want*.

Here is a summary of what I have said about buyer motivation:

1 There is a motive behind every human action.
2 There is always a prime motive and a subsidiary motive. The salesman, while concentrating on the prime motive, must never overlook the subsidiary motives.
3 Different buyers buy similar equipment, but often for different reasons. Selected motives should be used when applicable.

4   There are rational and emotional buying motives, and the importance of emotional motives must never be underrated.
5   The salesman's objective must always be to try to include in his sales offer the motivational force or forces which will impel the buyer to buy.
6   Buyers first fulfil *basic needs*, but often do not *recognise* their *real needs*.
7   Benefits should be 'personalised'.
8   A salesman turns *needs* into *wants* by proving benefits to the buyer or his company.

Benefits

Understanding buyer motivation means appreciating why and how he arrives at his decisions – why a buyer has a fear of change – and, most important, it enables a salesman to *progress an interview*. This means that while he is actually selling he will know, not by intuition but by sheer logic, how a buyer will react to claims, statements, offers; and appreciate the underlying thoughts of the buyer when objections are raised.

The professional salesman also knows that it is benefits derived from a knowledge of buyer motivation which act as a stimulus, and develop a want in the mind of the buyer.

5 Offer analysis

A salesman must be able to prove for himself that he is selling the right product, and offer analysis provides that proof, enabling him to identify *all* product features, and derive from them every single buyer benefit. It is the accumulation of these benefits which give proof of the value of the product. But it isn't enough to analyse a product alone. The analysis must be complete, embracing every factor which could influence a favourable decision.

For example, what will create buyer confidence?

A buyer cannot see the following in advance of purchasing: honesty, a fair deal, the backing given to guarantees (what is a guarantee worth if a company goes bankrupt?), completion of work on time, useful advertising campaigns, help during periods of shortages, more promotions, rapid service... Unless a customer believes that some or all of these assets exist, he may decide to buy from another supplier.

The small company

The salesman joining a newly formed or small company will soon appreciate the need for confidence-builders. Prospects may voice their fears by saying, 'Where are these in use? We have to be assured of continuity of supplies' or 'I'm not opening any new accounts'.

To overcome these fears of being let down on deliveries, of quality not being up to samples submitted, or of costly replacements, the sales offer must include confidence-building sentences based on company analysis:

> Our company has only been established about twelve months, but our managing director was for twenty years chief engineer with the largest electronics firm in America. It is his vast experience that has developed...

The larger company

Sales managers and salesmen with a large organisation sometimes believe that the good reputation of their company ensures the confidence of its customers for ever. This might be true if there were no competitors, which is a rare occurrence.

A salesman working for a market leader should still evolve confidence-building sentences, based on his offer analysis.

> Because of our wide ramifications, Mr Scotton, we can offer you a free survey. Our electronics engineer will come down here and evaluate ... The very size of our company enables us to give you a very special service. We have depots near all your branches; we keep stocks high to guarantee you immediate delivery ... Our company is sixty years old this month, but I know you will agree that it is very young in its outlook – always trying for better quality, better value...

Whether a company is large or small, there is always some aspect of its background which can be turned into a confidence-builder.

Even before analysing a product or service a salesman

should ask himself, *Why should a buyer have confidence in my company?* Surely not because of a claim to be the longest established, or the largest. *Old-established* may be a euphemism for old-fashioned. One pictures a series of medals on a company's headed notepaper, relics of exhibition awards in 1897, and then one thinks of obsolete plant, self-perpetuating directors and nepotism. *We are the largest* can mean a newly acquired member of a huge conglomerate, and conglomerates are only as good as the management teams of their diversified companies.

To discover true customer benefits the salesman must use the questioning technique, but the questions should be related not only to the product, but to the organisation of a company. Every fact, every feature must be analysed and the resulting benefits incorporated in the sales offer. That is why this chapter is called *Offer Analysis* and not Product Analysis. The objective of offer analysis is to identify and list every product feature, company advantage, advertising and promotional scheme, asset of company personnel, and then turn these features into benefits for the buyer.

Be selective

A complete analysis may result in the listing of 100 or more features, leading to 200 benefits. This is unusual, but it can happen, for example, when a salesman carries a wide range of component parts. However, a product analysis can result in perhaps ten features, twenty general benefits and thirty selective or personal benefits.

In many sales interviews a salesman can give his total sales offer, while at others he should be selective. The complete analysis provides a salesman with a store of features/benefits from which he can select those applicable to the buyer he is facing. The more thorough and complete the analysis, the better the salesman is able to select benefits which will motivate a buyer.

Another reason for the essential need of a complete analysis is to enable a salesman to evolve *double benefits*. If the salesman is selling to a retailer or whole-saler, or is calling on an architect, consulting engineer, or any other specifying authority, the 'buyer' is concerned with the needs of his clients/customers. He has to be sure that he is giving the best advice, that standards will be maintained, or that his customer will benefit from buying from him. In the sales offer, for example, a salesman calling on a retailer will incorporate in his offer a benefit to the buyer *and* his client.

That extra benefit

Firstly, remember again that when all things are equal, the orders are generally placed with the salesman a buyer likes and trusts the most. Secondly, it depends on your ability to find that *extra* benefit.

Picture now a pair of jockey scales, with the buyer occupying the jockey's seat and you replacing the weights. The buyer is listening to your sales offer and considering whether he should buy from you or not. These thoughts run through his mind:

> *Could I buy better elsewhere?*
> *Can I get a better price?*
> *Can I depend on deliveries?*
> *Can I rely on what this salesman promises?*
> *Will it break down?*
> *Will they be able to give immediate after-sales service?*
> *I don't think their locking device is as good as the one*
>   *I was shown last week.*

> *Perhaps I'd do better to rely on Company B – I know them well.*
> *I'd better think it over.*

All the time he is weighing up the proposal, the weight of his negative thoughts depressing his side of the scale. The odds move against your getting an order.

Then you begin to build strong benefits, and gradually the scale moves slightly in your favour. Eventually, to your great relief, as you add benefit upon benefit, your scale moves sharply down and the buyer's moves upwards.

At the tenth benefit the scales are equally poised. It is the moment of decision, but still the buyer hesitates – and while he is undecided you add one more benefit. It might only be of marginal importance, almost gossamer light in weight: '*The second-hand value keeps high, Mr. Brown. In five years' time we can offer you. . .*'

Your offer might be of small moment to the buyer, but it is fractionally more than the figure suggested by a competitor, although insignificant compared to the total offer. To your delight you hear the buyer saying, 'Perhaps it will do the job. The order is yours'.

The scale has been only slightly tilted – so slightly – in your favour. But it is enough.

We have been told by salesmen that they have often remembered this story when the going was hard, and it reminded them *always* to look for that extra benefit to beat competition.

Now you might ask, 'But if I've worked so hard on the offer analysis, how can I possibly find an *extra* benefit?' There is always one extra benefit. The effort to find it is worth while.

Imagine your life depended on squeezing an orange dry with your hands. You are handed a medium-sized orange and told that if one drop of juice is left, your life will be forfeit; so you begin to squeeze, relax, squeeze

again, relax, exert more pressure and squeeze even
harder. . . Finally, with aching hands and tired muscles,
you believe you have succeeded. You feel safe.

Looking down at the inert, misshapen, dry mass of
useless pulp, you hear the voice of the executioner
saying, 'It is not enough!' With fear sapping your
strength you make a final, determined effort. You
squeeze and squeeze again. Nothing happens. You take
a deep breath and exert every ounce of pressure. . .
One more drop of juice slowly drips from the pulp.

Squeezing the orange has a message for all salesmen.
Your livelihood and an important order could depend
on your ability to *squeeze* that extra benefit from the
product.

To do this you must think again of buying motivation
– rational and emotional reasons why people buy –
checking each feature again against each motivator.
You may have overlooked the emotional appeal of
pride, the rational appeal of security, or some tiny
aspect in the history of your company which will give
additional confidence to the buyer. You must find that
extra benefit.

Telling isn't selling

Many industrial salesmen use words, sentences, and expressions, and make statements which apparently offer
benefits but have no impact on the buyer. For example:

> *It will increase your profit.*
> *It will do a marvellous job.*
> *It is self-cleaning.*
> *Everyone is delighted with the results.*
> *We can deliver them right away.*
> *Our service is first-class.*
> *They are sold all over the world.*

There are hundreds of these superlatives which sound fine to the salesman, but factual statements do not personalise a benefit – and it is personal benefits which motivate a buyer. Salesmen therefore need a constant reminder to explain benefits in terms of the buyers' interests.

You will never forget to personalise benefits if you will always remember these three link words: *which mean that.*

They are sold all over the world is a confidence-building sentence used by many salesmen. By adding the words *which means that* it can be considerably strengthened: 'They are sold all over the world, *which means that* your agents can get immediate service'.

We *maintain large stocks* ... what does that mean? How large are the stocks? The word *large* can be interpreted differently by different people. How much stronger when a salesman says, 'We maintain large stocks, *which means that* we can almost take over your inventory problems, and, like others of our customers, you will cut down on stocks by 30 per cent or more, because we deliver so quickly'.

By using the words *which means that* you will be certain to give the benefit 'YOU' appeal, the YOU of course being the buyer. Every sale must have YOU appeal.

Here are some instances from companies using this Tack formula.

Sketchley Ltd – Sketchley Overall Service

'Ours is a complete service, *which means that* we take over all the problems of having stocks of the right size and type to satisfy you and your employees.'

Pinchin Johnson & Associates Ltd – Decorative Paint Division

'This aluminium paint incorporates highly polished

leafing aluminium in a silicone medium, and will be unaffected by heats of up to 1000°F, *which means that* if this material is used on your exhaust stacks, their appearance will be maintained for a much longer time than with conventional paints.'

Spillers Ltd – Animal Feed

'Our Calf Cudlets have been designed to replace a whole milk diet via early weaning, *which means that* the calf can be reared more cheaply, with less labour, and with reduced incidence of nutritional upset.'

L.M. van Moppes & Sons (Diamond Tools) Ltd

'This is a new design in diamond wheel-dressing tools. Its purchase price is much in line with ordinary-price dressers. It is, however, intended to be used to destruction without the necessity of resetting, *which means that* fewer tools need to be stocked to cover the resetting time, and also the machine operator spends less time changing his diamond.'

Drake & Fletcher Ltd – Engineers

'The centrifugal fan used only on Victair sprayers is far quieter than all competitive types of sprayer, *which means that* there is far less fatigue for the operator.'

Yardley & Co Ltd – Perfumiers and Fine Soap Makers

'You will see that our talcum powder is packed in a new plastic container. It is light and easy to handle, unbreakable and rust-proof, *which means that* the true fragrance of the talc is preserved for much longer than if any other form of packaging were used.'

Blick Time Recorders Ltd

'This is a Blick fully-automatic one-hand-operated electric card system time recorder, printing lateness and overtime in red for rapid analysis in your accounts department, *which means that* there is no time wasted. Staff clock in and out without delays or fumbling; they just put the card in the machine, and the rest is automatic.'

I & R Morley Ltd – Hosiery Manufacturers

'This underwear is made from fabric knitted in such a way that it produces efficient insulating properties, *which means that* the garment is suitable for both summer and winter.'

Slazenger Ltd – Sports Goods Manufacturers

'In the old days tennis balls started smooth and wore even smoother, so that control in play was very much more difficult. The Slazenger tennis ball is covered with a specially developed cloth called TW, or tennis weave – a combination of wool and nylon – *which means that* it will wear in new ball condition for hours of play.'

Lansing Bagnall Ltd – Fork Truck and Towtractor Manufacturers

'With this truck you will reduce your gangways to six feet, *which means that* you will store twenty per cent more material in this warehouse.

Here is an example of how a salesman can begin to work out his feature/benefit/YOU appeal for a specific type of fork-lift truck:

Features: uses diesel oil or LP Gas.
Benefits
1   No need to recharge battery.
2   No need for battery replacements.
3   No depending on electrical means for recharging
     batteries.
4   Gives maximum performance all the time

All these facts are derived from only one feature of the
fork-lift truck. There could of course be many more.
  Now let us give these facts YOU appeal:

1   No need for recharging batteries, *which means that*
     YOU will increase the workload without increasing
     costs. That is quite a saving.
2   No need for battery replacements, *which means that*
     YOU will cut costs.
3   YOU will not be dependent on electric mains for
     recharging the batteries, *which means that* your staff
     will not have to waste time moving away to an
     electrical junction, or running a cable. They can use
     the truck anywhere, at any time – a huge advantage
     in a very busy factory like yours.
4   YOU will get the maximum performance all
     the time, *which means that* running costs are
     cheaper.

Offer analysis sheet

To achieve the objectives of listing features/benefits/
YOU appeal and remembering *which means that*, a
simple offer analysis sheet can be used. This sheet helps
the salesman to organise his knowledge of his product
or service in such a way that it becomes easy to link
features to benefits, and then express these as personal

benefits, with the relevant YOU appeal. As many sheets as necessary may be used. Examples of Offer Analysis sheets completed by delegates attending our courses are included in the Appendix beginning on page 247.

6 Reach for the stars

At one of our earlier courses I asked some silly questions. I said, 'Put up your hands all those who want to be below-average salesmen'.

Naturally not one hand hit the air.

Then I said, 'And how many of you want to be average salesmen?'

Hands remained clasped.

'How many of you', I then asked, 'want to be just a bit above average?'

Quite a few hands pointed towards the ceiling.

Finally, I said, 'How many of you want to be top ranking star salesmen – leaders within your company?'

All the other hands shot up.

'Excellent!' I said. 'But let's think it through – and no show of hands, this time. How many of you will be willing to pay the price to become such a star?'

A price most certainly has to be paid – continual study of the work you do, getting back to basics over and over again... Only a few top golfing professionals make a lot of money. They are the stars; the others only think they ought to be stars. The winners spend long hours practising, sometimes following a long day of playing, while the losers may have hurried to the clubhouse to tell their tales of bad luck and relax over a drink.

Top athletes run for miles every day of every week, and for weeks on end. Lesser men excuse themselves from such sweated labour by insisting that it makes them stale, or that they will reach their peak too early.

Let us consider authors. On receiving those heart-breaking notes beginning *The Editor regrets. . .* the star doesn't curse and blame inefficient editors, but tears up the manuscript and starts all over again. Others give up.

The star becomes a star by doing so many of the things that the average person will quickly make excuses for *not* doing.

Now let us consider how star salesmen are able to win over many difficult buyers and turn that uninterested prospect into one who is very much interested in the salesman's products. How does the star salesman show his strength, his determination? How does he discipline himself?

A complete offer analysis may be developed with loving care and attention, meticulous in every detail – the continual squeezing of the orange to find that *extra* benefit. But the salesman may still feel, or rather remain, average if he doesn't obey the rules which apply to star quality.

I was eighteen when I learned a lesson which turned me into a much better salesman. It could do the same for you!

I have already mentioned it briefly. It is known as *conversational selling*.

At that time I was an agent selling office stationery, sharing an office with a Frenchman, André Simon. He was an agent for a Lyons silk manufacturer, and always did extremely well, while I always seemed to be doing extremely badly in comparison. Everyone told me that Simon was a great salesman.

One day I asked him whether I could accompany him on some of his sales visits. He agreed, and we called on several buyers that day.

I listened and I wondered. It all seemed so easy! If an

objection was raised, it seemed to be in the realm of information-seeking rather than to avoid buying.

The objection I used to receive regularly at that time was, 'We are well satisfied with our present suppliers'. I never seemed to be able to overcome that, but when a similar objection was raised with Simon, it was not brushed aside, it was just talked away. Buyers seemed so interested in the benefits that Simon extolled; orders closed themselves so naturally. At the end of the day I was none the wiser.

I had witnessed a magician at work, but I still couldn't fathom how the tricks were performed.

Back in our office in Argyll Street, next to the London Palladium, I said, 'You make it all sound so easy – but then, you have such a marvellous range of silk fabrics'.

Simon smiled and said, 'That, I know. But my competitors from Lyons also have splendid ranges of fabrics. Buyers have to be motivated to give us the business'.

These of course were not the exact words used, but they are near enough, and were spoken with his delightful French accent. I remember him elegantly lighting a cigarette. I at that time couldn't even do that gracefully.

'But you are young', he went on, 'and you will make the mistakes of youth.'

I bridled. 'I can't accept that. I've had lots of experience.'

He shrugged his shoulders. 'So, you are experienced. But you are still failing – and yet the solution is simple. It happens to most young salesmen in the early days of their career, and a great many experienced salesmen as well! You have a good personality, a command of the language – all you have to do is to stop selling.'

I was stunned! Did he mean that I ought to give up my career in salesmanship?

Noticing my expression, Simon continued, 'I only mean stop being a typical salesman so that you can then become a very good salesman'.

My expression changed to one of perplexity.

'Let me explain', said Simon. 'The name "buyer" is a misnomer. Buyers dislike buying, except of course when they place orders for repeat business. They are so afraid of making a mistake.'

'And what makes them fearful?'

'Being sold to by a salesman – hearing the selling jargon, stereotyped sentences, which tell them that a salesman is engaged in his persuasive work.

'If you stop selling and become a good conversationalist, you will win more often than you will lose. You must always be a salesman first, but salesmanship must be combined with conversational selling. And your customer must never see the demarcation line.

'And that's it. Sell conversationally and you will become a far better salesman.'

'How do I do that?' I asked.

Simon replied, 'It isn't easy – in fact, it's quite difficult. Conversational selling, basically, means selling to the professional buyer as you would if you were a personal friend; a friend, for example, whom you want to persuade to join a club, or to change his holiday plans to fit in with yours. . .

'In these selling situations you would not sound like a cut-from-the-pattern salesman.

'Here is a more simple explanation: When answering objections, you will often use an apparent agreement technique. Why? First, to relax the buyer, which will make your response to the objection all the stronger.

'I can buy more cheaply', says the buyer.

'The salesman's immediate response should be, "I agree" – a pause, "BUT. . ."' He will then follow by giving the reason why the buyer can be mistaken in his judgement that he can buy more cheaply.

'But if you were trying to convince a friend to visit
Cyprus with you on holiday, and he objected, saying,
"I'm not happy with Cyprus, it's too hot there", you
wouldn't snap back "I agree, but..." You would
probably say something like, "Yes John, you certainly
have a point there. It is really hot at that time of the
year. But John" – a pause, then, "Look at it this way".

'You would then explain why the heat would not
affect him because of the swimming pool – the shaded
areas – the sunshades, etc. It would all be a part of a
friendly conversation.'

Subsequently I learned one of the main reasons why
Simon was so successful at conversational selling. It
may surprise salesmen, but buyers do tense before
signing an order. The salesman has to take away that
tension, and relax the buyer, and he can do so by selling
conversationally – and by being relaxed himself.

The other day I was in the men's department of a
well-known store. I stopped in my journey to the
hairdressing section to look through a tie rack. Nearby
a salesman was using all his selling skills to persuade a
customer to buy an expensive cashmere ready-made
coat.

I could sense that customer's fears. The price was so
high. What would his wife say about it? I could almost
read the customer's mind as he tried to think of an
excuse for moving away.

The salesman, quite unaware of the tension he was
creating, continued with his patter: 'It looks tailormade
on you, sir. Let me show you the back in this mirror'.
(Why are all such assistants so much more concerned
with backs than with fronts?) But to no avail. The
customer was already beginning to take the coat off.

Nearby another gentleman was studying another
coat, accompanied by a lady whom I assumed to be his
wife. Suddenly she turned, saw the customer near me in
the cashmere coat, and said loudly, 'That's the one you

want, Arthur. It's very smart. And it's your colour, too!'

The customer in the cashmere coat hesitated, eased the coat back on again, and looked in the mirror, preening himself and turning this way and that as the tension drained from him. Those few words of approval were all that he needed.

The salesman, if he had learned conversational selling, could have used the same words to similar effect.

Do, please, remember then: a tense buyer doesn't buy, and you can relax a buyer by talking in a conversational manner.

It isn't easy to switch from platitudes to conversational selling. Hard work is needed to break the mould. At every interview you will have to will yourself to imagine talking to a friend, but without the familiarity.

Simon was so right! I eventually solved the problem by learning to relax myself, because Simon had told me that conversational selling and relaxation go together.

We used to teach relaxation exercises at our courses, but no longer do so because research showed that too many delegates would not bother to carry out the exercises daily for a period of three months.

But here is a short cut to relaxation, while selling:

1 Relax the facial muscles. A smile helps, so long as it is a relaxed smile.
2 Then relax the body by letting the shoulders drop.

These two tips can help you to relax, provided that at the same time as you relax your shoulders you mutter to yourself, 'Let go', and let your muscles go. There is no long-term benefit, but it does work in the short term.

I once asked several successful executives each to give an example of a lesson they learned when selling which had helped them during their career.

A. S. J. Painter, then managing director of E. R. Howard, the Three-in-One oil people, told me how he succeeded in spite of his manager's certainty that he would fail:

I was promoted to a territory in Lancashire as assistant to a field manager who didn't want an assistant, and if he had to have one, he didn't want that assistant to succeed.

On my first day out he hand-picked for me a number of hopeless customers to visit. My enthusiasm carried me through.

At lunch time I met the manager.

'How did you get on?' he asked me.

'How many calls did you make?'

'Fifteen', I said.

'Good heavens!' he said. 'Nobody could make that many calls and get orders.'

'But I did', I replied. 'I got twelve orders.'

'How many?' my supervisor asked incredulously. 'Twelve!'

He thought for a moment, then said, 'I don't suppose they'll stick'.

But they did stick.

That day's work paved the way for me to executive status. Its value lay in its lessons, which were threefold.

Firstly, enthusiasm can sell where jaded experience will be daunted.

Secondly, no prospect should be written off in advance.

And thirdly, the man who makes the calls gets the results.

Summed up, his words of advice were: *Give me enthusiasm and cheerfulness, and I'll conquer the world!*

D. W. Barrett, CBE, then director and general manager of Smith's Clocks and Watches, gave me this example:

Always set yourself an objective – a definite goal or target – and never forget it. Always have it in mind, and let every action on your part be directed towards it.

To the young, ambitious salesman, I would say, 'Set out to become the finest salesman in the world, and whilst pursuing this aim, first endeavour to become the finest salesman in your firm – then in your industry, always pursuing, always achieving. Never, never waver. Make sure your objective will be achieved.

P. A. Brown, then director of National Cash Registers Ltd., gave this advice:

I had just missed an order. I sensed victory, but didn't achieve it.

I left Mr Johnson, the customer and slumped myself down behind the wheel of my car, fed up. My finger was on the gear lever, ready to hasten away, when a thought swept through my brain.

'You left out the best bit!' I said to myself. 'You're an ass! You forgot to talk about individual responsibility where money is concerned.'

I swore at myself as I wrote down in my notebook several of the points I should have mentioned while I was still in the shop.

Then I went back. 'Mr. Johnson', I said, 'I must be slipping. I didn't clear up that point about. . .'

I got the order – a far larger one than I had been hoping I was going to get.

All salesmen should remember to tell the full story at every call. I mentioned this earlier, as you know, but I thought the extra proof provided by Mr. Brown would help to convince you.

From George Drexler, then chairman and managing Director of Ofrex Ltd, came this advice:

In all that you do and think, you must be sincere and honest – not only to your prospects, customers, and management, but first of all, to yourself. Remember always, you may be working for a company, but first and foremost, you are working for yourself. You work for your own satisfaction, for your advancement, so that you may improve your standard of living and that of your family.

Whenever anyone in selling gets the feeling that he can fool a customer, or his sales manager, he is mistaken. In the end – and this may take him some time to find out – he discovers that the only man to be fooled is himself.

The three ingredients for honour and satisfaction are: *sincerity, integrity, and honesty.*

A. B. Lamont, then branch manager of Manufacturers Life Insurance Company of Canada, had this advice to offer:

Many salesmen spend a lot of time considering their lost sales, and telling their supervisors and colleagues the reasons why the sale was lost.

Strangely, they seldom take the trouble to analyse the reasons why they have been successful in the sales they have made.

Every sale can help a salesman to further successes, if he will only search for the reasons why the customer bought.

F. W. Beckley, then managing director of Shredded Wheat Co. Ltd, had this to say:

In the word *business* there is the letter U and the letter I – and the U comes before the I. The I is silent.

This, you should remember not only when you make the approach, but right throughout the sale.

Use the word *I* as little as you can, but use the

word *you* as often as possible. And when using the word *you*, let the prospect or customer hear his own name. No one ever tires of hearing his own name.

Bruce Goodman, when managing director of Marks & Spencer, told me that a weakness of many of the salesmen who call on them was that they strive to be cleverer than the buyers technically.

His advice was: *don't be too brilliant. You could undermine the authority and importance of the buyer.*

R. J. Stafford, a New York insurance broker, told me he learned a lesson when he overheard a salesman calling on the manager of a shop. After a few minutes the salesman had said, 'Mr. Harvey, you must have had a most interesting career building up this business. How did you start?'

Stafford told me that that was a wonderful lesson. The way to win a man over to your way of thinking is to let him talk about himself, and one way to do that is to ask him how he started in business.

B. J. Evershed, then managing director of Eversheds, the well-known suppliers of stationery and calendars, had this advice for salesmen:

Be a *go-giver* rather than a go-getter. You can always give understanding, politeness, the benefit of your skills. You can give praise, your attention, or good service. You can give sympathy and understanding, you can give experience, you can give friendship. . .

Go-givers succeed more often than the so-called whiz-kid go-getters.

Victor Barnard buys for a group of chain stores, and spends five days a week seeing salesmen. When asked what irritated him most about salesmen, he answered:

Salesmen who lean on my desk. Those who let their

eyes wander all over the papers on my desk, as if seeking some private information. Men who will keep scratching a spot on their face or their head. Men who talk too much. And worse of all, those who try to impress me with their great importance.

Lastly, from me. When making a sale, make sure that you don't do more than 60 per cent of the talking. Let the prospect do the other 40 per cent, and when he is talking, be a good listener – a silent listener. Don't be thinking about what you are going to say next. Don't interrupt.

Confucius said, *When you listen you learn*. When a salesman learns to listen, he sells more.

Sell your way to success

Let us return to Chapter 3, The right mental attitude, and read it again. Reread this chapter also.

The chapters to follow, on techniques, you will master with ease and readily apply – they are so logical. But the changing of yourself and your way of thinking, that is much more difficult.

You will cope, by doing your own thing, by paying lip service to self-motivation. But if you want to become a star and to be respected as a star, then you have to make that extra journey – that journey which, as Donne said, *will involve you in mankind*.

There is no easy road to success, but it is the one you can take. In life we have all been given the right to choose, and the choice now is yours.

Before we move on to the skills, consider all the advice you have been given. Then indulge in a modicum of self-analysis, and you are on your way to stardom.

7 The ABC of selling

At times everyone uses a sales presentation, although quite unaware of doing so. The person who visits a bank manager for a loan rehearses and rehearses every word of his plea for cash, when confronted by that grim-faced, dour, depressing man. A good presentation will bring quite a change in the manager's demeanour. A smile will appear, the dourness and depression depart. The would-be borrower who does not give deep thought to a logical presentation may find it difficult to persuade a bank manager to grant him a loan.

When Mrs Hall tells Mr Hall to ask the boss for a rise in salary, together they will rehearse the words to be used. 'And don't forget to tell him. . .' says Mrs Hall – and tell him Mr Hall will, in the hope of presenting his boss with a well-thought-out argument.

All salesmen use presentations. Some are bad, some average, some good, some excellent. Your aim is to ensure that your presentation is excellent.

Even when a salesman sees many different buyers daily, or calls back regularly on them, a presentation can still be adapted for each call. No sales offer should fail through the inability of the buyer to understand it, and to appreciate how it can benefit him and his business.

The presentation has to be honed to perfection for each call – a slight change here, more important change there, perhaps because of the introduction of a new product or new service which would apply to a particular buyer.

Another point to remember is that when you have worked out a very good sales presentation, or sales sequence, keep to it. Would a Shakespearean actor decide to alter the lines of a play on different nights, because he felt that they would have greater audience appeal?

That's nonsense, isn't it? One doesn't tamper with perfection, or even near perfection.

The only adaptions which do take place in a presentation are of course when calling back regularly on customers. But a presentation must be prepared for every visit to a buyer – first or tenth.

The original presentation, or sales sequence, as it was then called, originated in the USA. It was called *The Monologue*.

We first encountered it on a visit to Chicago when we attended an induction course of a cash register company. The new salesmen were expected to memorise word for word a thirty-four-page sales story, which subsequently had to be repeated verbatim. A very experienced actor might have managed it, given enough cues, but the salesmen in that course were given only ten days to enable them to memorise every line of the story.

The theory behind the monologue (which is still used by any number of direct selling companies) was: *Don't tamper with perfection.* I remember the instructor saying, 'Why try to improve on a sequence which we have researched, tested, and found to be the best way to sell our cash registers? We have formulated for you the right way to sell at every call – the right way for each of you to earn a high income – so why change a word?'

He then went on, 'If you do change a word, then next you will be changing two words – then three, and on and on until you have moved right away from the tested means to succeed. Why use second best, when you can use the best?'

Let me say right away, it worked for them at the time. It still works for telephone salesmen, who use prepared scripts. But although we saw then the logic of the argument, we formed an immediate distaste for it. To us it was too near brain-washing, and made no provision for personality differences or initiative.

Well, that is not quite right. The facts always remain the same, and must never be changed. It is the persuasive padding which can make the difference between a good presentation and a very ordinary one.

If it were possible to sell simply by stating facts, no salesmen would be needed. Every order could be taken by post.

It is right to think inexperienced recruits will mostly fail, if left to develop their own presentation. It is wrong in the respect that a parrotwise sales sequence is not the answer to problems caused by inexperience. So what must be formulated in the mind of every salesman is a presentation which can be memorised, yet combines with the salesman's own personality and initiative, resulting in the full presentation being given at every call.

At the other extreme are the companies who advertise for, and engage, salesmen with experience. Such salesmen are expected to succeed, because of their years of selling. That, too, is wrong.

Both experienced and inexperienced salesmen benefit from a plan which enables a sales presentation to be given in logical sequence, with no salient features omitted. Such a sequence must allow for a salesman to elaborate, give personal proof stories, and use his brochures effectively, including all those human relation factors which can motivate a buyer.

What it must not do is tie a salesman rigidly to a set

of words. Yet it must provide key sentences which never seem stale from repetition but can always be personalised.

In the early days we broke the sales sequence down into steps: (1) the Approach, (2) Creation of Interest, (3) Creation of Confidence, (4) Creating the Desire, etc., until the Close was reached. But long experience in training our own staff, as well as thousands of salesmen who pass through our courses every year, has taught us that such steps can mislead a salesman.

Why have one selling step for creating confidence, when it should be created all the way through the sale, starting with the salesman's appearance, his approach, and so on?

There must be creation of interest at the approach stage, but it must be maintained throughout the sale. To have one step only for creating interest gives the impression that one can be uninteresting throughout other parts of the sequence.

What we also discovered over a period of time was that a sales presentation is only a presentation of benefits – benefits at the approach, benefits by confidence-building, benefits during the close, and a number of benefits in between. All the salesman has to do therefore is to consider how to present his benefits in a logical sequence, based on the offer analysis forms.

We did try the monologue sequence for a long time when training our own sales staff. We did not find it worked effectively, for the reasons given.

We then tried a duologue sales presentation, which allowed for responses from the buyer to questions put by the salesmen, and to points raised by the salesmen. That didn't succeed either, so we moved on to the selling sentence technique, based on benefits and more benefits, until we simplified the whole procedure of building a sales presentation. At our instruction courses today we only teach three steps: the Approach, How to Present Benefits, and the Close.

I am sure that you will now appreciate the value of the offer analysis sheets, to enable you not only to be logical in your presentation, but also to work out a good approach and a good close. On those sheets, remember, are listed every conceivable benefit accruing to the buyer if he decides to purchase your product or service. You cannot provide a last-minute additional benefit, because you have researched so deeply, and concentrated every fact relating to your product which can be turned into a benefit.

But adjustments have to be made. The sequence may change according to a buyer's likes or prejudices – when new products are introduced, or new advertising campaigns launched. Even if nothing new has been introduced, you will still change a sequence around, depending largely on what happened at a previous visit.

The strong salesman

What is meant by strength in selling? It surely isn't table-thumping, shouting, change of features, gesticulating... A salesman's strength can only be shown through the words he uses.

Words

There are many aids to person-to-person selling; sales brochures, demonstration models, samples, film strips, photographs and drawings, all play their part. But while such sales aids definitely help a salesman, if the salesman doesn't speak, he will not sell. If it were possible to market without person-to-person selling, the company would sell by direct mail.

The salesman then is paid to talk. Many a salesman

has made a living without using a single sales aid; but few salesmen could succeed if they did not make use of the right words at the right time. A salesman lives by the words he uses and he shows strength through the words he uses. The weak salesman uses words such as 'I wonder', 'I think', 'I hope', 'Possibly' ... A salesman shows strength by saying, 'I am sure that', 'I know', 'It will...' All these words can be used because you have confidence in your products. If you haven't this confidence, you should not be selling them.

A salesman succeeds because he uses *positive* words, not negative, words, but he does not use these words in isolation. They are strung together to become compelling sentences, and every sentence should motivate the mind of the buyer towards accepting his offer.

But how to remember these compelling sentences?

Key sentences

A selling sentence is one which is related to a feature of the product and will call to mind the form of illustration needed to convince and motivate the buyer. Throughout life we are reminded of what is to follow by such sentences as 'Early to bed, early to rise' – need I tell you the next few words? If you were selling you would elaborate on the ways in which the buyer could be healthier, wealthier, and, in a circumspect manner, wiser.

Once a key sentence is remembered, it is almost impossible to stop the flow of words that will build and elaborate on that sentence.

'A bird in the hand...' I wouldn't mind betting that through your mind there immediately flashed the words 'is worth two in the bush'. In exactly the same way, if you use such a selling sentence as 'It will turn an eight-hour day into an eight-hour *working* day', it will immediately elaborate and explain how your product or service will provide continuity of operation.

Here are some more examples, provided by delegates at our courses.

A salesman is selling a new external paint. The paint has a very important feature eliminating the need for a lot of preparatory work, including priming and sealing. An easily remembered key sentence could be *You don't have to prime or seal*, which highlights the obvious benefits of:

1 *Saving time* – important in factory maintenance.
2 *Saving labour* – a very big benefit indeed where maintenance labour is scarce.
3 *Saving materials* – a primer and paint in one tin.
4 *A considerable saving on the hire of scaffolding*.

With that single, easily remembered sentence, a salesman can pinpoint the YOU appeal so vital to his presentation.

A salesman offering catering services to industry could use this sentence: *Quality meals for your staff under your own roof*. These few words remind the salesman of the many factors which could show benefits to the buyer:

1 The *quality* of the meals, which would ensure no complaints.
2 The *consistency* of the service.
3 The *efficiency* that backs it.
4 The dangers of staff having to go out at midday, skipping meals, and therefore producing less work during the afternoon (own roof).
5 Staff who go out and arrive back late because of the difficulty of getting a meal locally (own roof).
6 The effect on staff of seeing that the management have their interests at heart (quality).

7   The retention of key personnel because of this
    additional welfare (your staff).
8   Easier recruitment through offering extra facilities.

An excellent key sentence used by Dunlop is: *Dunlop Thixofix spreads like butter – grips like iron.* After voicing that sentence no salesman could fail to describe vividly the ease of application, as well as the many uses of Thixofix.

Building positive sentences will enable you to memorise a complete series of benefits. Enjoy yourself – and we all enjoy being creative – by working out key sentences while driving the car, or watching bad television.

Remembering the benefit sequence, a salesman will be able to present his case to the buyer in a logical, clear, and progressive manner, while avoiding the constrictions of a rigid sales formula.

We believe that although a sales training manager may provide his salesmen with guidelines, he should not attempt to put a set of words into their mouths. A salesman must evolve his own sentences, his own manner of elaborating the facts derived from these key words.

It is very hard to ape others, whereas it is easy to remember those sentences which we have originated ourselves. A salesman should sell conversationally, and present his facts in a logical order by memorising key sentences.

Mind reading

When we were in our twenties, my brother was a highly skilled amateur magician, much in demand by charitable organisations. We used to do a double act of mind-reading, which baffled everyone. Lines from

books, produced at random, were apparently tele-
pathically passed from one of us to the other; but it was
all a trick – although at that time people were quite
certain that, as brothers, there was some strange tele-
pathy between us.

All mind-reading acts are tricks of the magical trade.
Mind-reading doesn't exist.

After living with someone for years, or meeting
someone regularly, one can draw certain conclusions as
to how they may think or act under certain circumstances, but even that is only 50 per cent right, because
people change their minds so quickly about every subject under the sun – except the one with which they
are emotionally concerned at the time. So never try to
read a buyer's mind. By asking questions one can get
some idea of the way he is thinking, but that we shall
cover later.

However, there is one simple means whereby you
can answer every single query that is likely to come to
his mind while you are selling to him: *make certain that
you give a full presentation at every call*. Never cut or
discard because *you* feel he will not be interested. I can
cite case after case of salesmen who have shortened
their presentation, only to discover at a subsequent visit
that a competitor has called, emphasised the omissions,
and has clinched the order. The first salesman only
paves the way for a competitor, when he does not stress
every benefit, which is the only way to ensure that there
will be no unanswered questions in the mind of the
buyer.

Remember then: *Cover all the ground – all the
benefits – at every call.*

Forgive the repetition, but sometimes repetition is
essential to drive home an important message.

8 The approach

The opening of the presentation is designed to obtain
and hold the attention of the buyer. Subsequently, all
the words and actions of the salesman should so maintain the interest that the only closing technique needed
is a gentle nudge.

The first consideration is not so much what will hold
the buyer's attention as what might stop him giving us
his full attention when we first meet.

Let us be the buyer for a moment. We meet someone
for the first time and immediately find him unlikeable,
likeable, or nondescript – and we arrive at that
conclusion within seconds of an introduction, without
any real knowledge of the other person.

It's all summed up in the romantic novels – love at
first sight, across a crowded room. That is not something which happens only in fiction.

A friend of mind told me that he had decided to
marry for the second time when he saw a woman
dancing with another man. At that time he turned to his
companion and said, 'There's the woman I'm going to
marry!' – and he did.

Such is the power of personal appearance, manner,
bearing, chemistry – call it what you will! You will
agree that we do make up our minds quickly to like or
dislike.

In the selling world, dislikes can turn into 'stoppers' –
a switch-off by the buyer. Let us consider some of

these stoppers, which can occur within the first few seconds of a meeting.

Stopper No. 1

An almost certain stopper is to attempt to sell under adverse conditions. A salesman can generate such conditions for himself, by arriving in a buyer's office with a very wet macintosh and an even wetter umbrella, then not knowing whether to take off the mac or where to park the umbrella.

This most certainly inhibits the opening remarks of that salesman.

A salesman should always try to leave a macintosh, coat, umbrella, or hat outside the buyer's office – in a waiting room, on a chair... The chances of their theft are probably 500 to 1 – a chance well worth taking.

Stopper No. 2

Usually adverse conditions are created by the buyer himself. If you are calling on a shopkeeper while he is dressing his window, say, or busy with a customer, or checking his stocks, the chances of getting a good order are remote. Either stand aside and wait for things to quieten down – if you know the customer well, you can perhaps suggest that you wait in his office for him – or call back.

He may call out to you, 'Repeat the same again', or words to that effect, but you are not there on a goodwill mission, you are there to sell, and that verbal order may not be good enough. You must try very hard to interview the shopkeeper when he can devote his whole attention to you.

Stopper No. 3 – On the shop floor

Here is a story told to us by a delegate attending one of our courses:

He had called to see a works director, but arrived before the appointed time, to be told that the director was talking to some of his operators in A shop. The delegate went down to A shop, and saw the director in deep conversation with some machine operators. He quickly realised that a controversial discussion was taking place. The director, noticing him said, 'I won't be long.'

He was then faced with the alternative of waiting for the director to see him later or making an appointment for another occasion. He did not attempt to read the director's mind, because he knew that if they met later, the man's mind would still be troubled by the controversial situation on the shop floor. He therefore returned to the director's office, saw the secretary, and left with her a note to the effect that he realised the director was extremely busy and under pressure, and he did not think it would be fair for him to stay and take up his time under these circumstances. He then arranged an appointment for later with the secretary.

That delegate told us that he obtained a large order on his subsequent call, but he was sure that he would not have won that order if he had stayed and attempted to sell under the adverse conditions.

Stopper No. 4 – Selling in company

Sometimes a salesman will call at an appointed time, only to find that the buyer is surrounded by assistants, colleagues, or other employees. The atmosphere seems quite friendly and the salesman, in these circumstances, may stay to sell in front of the audience.

Avoid doing that if at all possible. It can be a stopper.

Under these conditions, almost inevitably, the buyer will show off in front of his staff to build his own importance – he is sarcastic, say, asks foolish questions, or acts dictatorially, which he would never do if he were on his own. Employees will also add their comments. Some will be for, some against – mostly against, if they sense that they are echoing the views of their chief.

This is an entirely different situation from selling to committees, when all those present are participants in the buying situation. The salesman is aware of the committees' structure, and knows how to deal with each of those present.

I remember one occasion when I was invited by a buyer to join him and some colleagues for lunch in the factory canteen. At that time I felt very proud that the offer had been made; but when, over lunch, I was questioned, and some of my answers were treated rather lightly, I realised that I was selling under very bad conditions. I never let that happen again.

Stopper No. 5 – Not outside the office

You are on your way to meet Mr Ainsworth, the buyer, when he emerges from his office and meets you in the corridor. He says, 'You're just the man I wanted to see! You assured me last week when you called that our delivery requests would be met, but we have been held up on the shop floor because...'

What should you do? Do you answer his query there and then? Do you immediately introduce the new equipment you want to talk about to him? Do you take out your brochures in the corridor?

If you do, you may be selling under adverse conditions. You have to be strong and say to Mr Ainsworth,

'You don't want excuses, you want answers to your queries, and you also want to know about the new development which will certainly cut down your production time. Can we go into your office for a few minutes, please? I'll just show you some drawings'.

What you must do then is walk towards the office door. Don't wait for a 'Yes' – move away, as if you are certain that Mr Ainsworth is agreeable to your request. If you stand still and wait for the buyer to say something, he may well say, 'No', or be non-committal. Many, many sales are lost in corridors and waiting rooms. They are buyer-generated adverse conditions – don't let the buyer get away with it. If you know that the conditions are against you, call back another day.

Stopper No. 6 – The stopper which is not a stopper

It isn't easy to make that instant decision as to whether conditions are adverse or not. When that shopkeeper looks very busy, is he really busy or is he making a lot of fuss about very little? When the buyer says, 'I can only spare you two or three minutes', is he telling you the truth?

It may be the buyer's plan to get rid of you before you start selling, or to make certain that he is going to get rid of you within two or three minutes. When in doubt, carry on selling. You will quickly discover whether you can hold the buyer's attention or not.

You will find, however, that in many cases when benefit follows benefit, the two-minute offer is forgotten.

Stopper No. 7 – The chat gap

It is not always the friendly buyer who is the one who places the orders. It may be the overbearing monster who becomes your best customer; but most buyers, whether they be managing director, manager, or professional buyer, are reasonable people, and will make the usual comments when approached by a salesman for the first time – 'How are you?', 'Did you have a problem getting here?', 'Has the strike affected you?' and so on.

When you call upon a customer regularly, then inevitably either he or you will refer to something outside business which has happened in the past. He may ask you, 'How did your boy get on with his exams?' or 'Did you have a good holiday?'

You have not uttered your approach sentence. You are talking about irrelevant matters, very much like the entertainer who warms up audiences before the chief entertainer arrives on the stage.

A salesman therefore cannot always speak that wonderful opening sentence he has formulated in his mind before the chat gap has ended. This applies particularly when a friendship has developed with a buyer over many years. The objective of the salesman, however, is to keep the chat gap short. To do so, never talk about yourself, your interests, your hobbies, holidays, family, health, garden, traffic problems, newspaper headlines, or the weather – or if you do have to, a few words are enough. When you are asked, 'Did you have a nice holiday?' – and this has been mentioned earlier in the book – the answer is, 'Yes, thank you'.

So many salesmen elaborate. The chat gap lengthens, and the selling time shortens. When a salesman is foolish enough to waste time by a chat gap, you may be sure that the buyer will switch off, and he may still be switched off when that polished opening sentence is spoken.

It is very hard for a salesman to learn this lesson. So often they have said to me, 'But it's different in my case, my buyers want to hear about. . .'

When I was once accompanying a book salesman from Herbert Jenkins, the publishers of my first novels, he told me in advance that all the buyers liked hearing his funny stories. We called on a shop in Aldershot and he told his funny stories. He didn't get much of an order. Later I called back on that shop again, because I was living in the area, and the shopowner said, 'Can't you do something about Mr Williams? He will tell me his bloody silly stories, and waste my time!' But the salesman wouldn't have believed me if I'd told him this.

The lesson is: a chat gap is purely a few seconds of polite introduction – nothing more. Don't make it last, or it will become a stopper.

Getting attention

Whether the chat gap lasts five seconds or five minutes, as soon as it ends, it is vital for the salesman to gain the buyer's attention, by interesting him in the opening of his sales offer. There are six proven techniques, each of which can enable a salesman to hold the buyer's attention time and time again. These techniques can be used at the first call or the tenth. They are:

(a) The factual opening.
(b) The question opening.
(c) The reference opening.
(d) The sales-aid opening.
(e) The demonstration opening.
(f) The link opening.

Factual opening

We all have an insatiable desire to learn facts about subjects which interest us. What other reason is there for the *Guinness Book of Records* becoming a world best-seller? If we are sending our child to a new school, all the facts we can gather about that school are read avidly. If someone is considering emigrating, he reads every fact he can about the country in which he hopes eventually to settle down. Just think of the brochures we study when we are planning a holiday abroad. We lap up the facts – six miles of sand, a hundred and fifty-two restaurants, eight golf courses, four swimming pools. . .

Why should buyers be any different in their thinking? We know that they are no different – that they are motivated in the same way as all of us. Buyers' attention can always be held by a fact, or a series of facts, if those facts are directly connected with their business; and that is just as true on the fiftieth call as on the first.

Here are some examples of factual openings:

1   'Mr Urquhart, it is a fact that oil fuels contain more energy in a given volume than any other fuel, but not all fuels are consistent and dependable. With X, we guarantee. . .'

2   'Very few companies need a huge hardware investment. It is a fact that most businesses only need day-to-day assistance for productive work in factory or office. Our new. . .'

3   'There has now been found a way of fixing very heavy objects to a cavity wall without having to use special plugs or studding. . .'

4   'Mrs Simpson, in a recent report from the World Health Council it was stated that noise was a main cause of stress in business. Our triple glazing will. . .'

5   'Mr McKay, you can now have up to 1,500 internal telephone extensions. As your plant covers so many acres I am sure you will be interested in our new. . .'

6   'It is an unfortunate fact, Mr Walton, as you know, that vandals are continually breaking factory windows on this estate. But it need not happen to your factory any more, because now, we have a new glass. . .'

7   'It is not generally known, Mrs Jennings, that one electric convection oven can cook 800 meals in eight minutes. . .'

8   'Good morning, Mr Lamb. With every expanding watch bracelet you sell there is a hidden extra 5 per cent profit for you. I am from the Jewellery Corporation. . .'

9   'Good morning, Mrs Delaney. I have been outside your shop for five minutes, during which time seventy-four people passed by – that is 888 every hour. Do you know that many more of them could be induced to stop and look in your window? I am from Window Display Limited, and we have. . .'

10   'Good morning, Mr Tinsley. It is a major expense, as you know, to send back faulty shirts to the manufacturers. At our factory returns are negligible because of our quality procedures. I am from the Best Shirt Company. . .'

11   'Good morning, Mrs MacBride. You can now have one photocopier, not only for all office duplicating but also to handle multiple runs, and special systems which used to require very expensive printing machine. I am from. . .'

12   'One of the difficulties of handling frozen foodstuffs is that the limited amount of storage space often restricts the varieties you can handle. My company, XYS Limited, has instituted a daily delivery scheme, using insulated vans, carrying every variety of frozen product . . .'

13   'Scaffolding equipment is usually required at short notice in the building trade, but only the larger builders can afford to buy adequate stocks.

> My company, XYZ Scaffolding Ltd, operates an
> extremely attractive rental scheme, with depots
> placed strategically throughout the country, to
> supply your needs within hours...'

The question opening

Only those facing interrogation refuse to answer questions. The rest of us do so with pleasure, either
instantly or after some thought.

When we are in a furniture shop and the assistant
says, 'What is the present colour scheme in your
bedroom?', we are eager to tell her the design of our
curtains, the colour of the carpet, the matching tones of
the upholstery and the wallpaper... One simple question leads us immediately into her sales offer.

If a car salesman asks us, 'Will you be using the car
abroad as well as in this country?', we can hardly wait
to tell him of our projected tour of the Continent.

Buyers always react to a question by becoming
caught up in the sale. Whether you have to influence
the mind of a purchasing manager, personnel officer,
shop foreman, design engineer, project manager – a
question will immediately produce his undivided attention. Do not be concerned, however, at the brevity of
his reply. Even if he only says 'Yes' or 'No', this still
allows you to elaborate, and you will have achieved
your objective.

Here are some examples:

'Mr Theobalds, is it right that from this factory you
export to nearly every part of the world?'
 'Yes, we're very proud of our exporting achievements.'
 'Then you will be interested to hear of our new daily
world wide cargo flights...'

'Mr Bowen, am I right in saying that it is essential for
you to use refrigerated vans for delivery?'

'Yes.'
'Then you will be interested in our. . .'

'Mr Laurie, I am sure you will agree that everyone, these days, should consider ways of reducing pollution.'
'Yes, I certainly agree with that.'
'Well, we have designed a revolutionary exhaust system to eliminate completely those intensely choking diesel fumes. Our new. . .'

'Mr Percival, is it right that one of your main problems is the risk of water getting into the bearings?'
'That's a problem we always have.'
'Well, our new plastic covered bearings can relieve you of that worry, because. . .'

'Miss King, can your present photocopier copy right up to the spine of a ledger?'
'No.'
'But you do think it would be helpful if it did?'
'Yes, on occasion perhaps.'
'Well, our new Fotoit will. . .'

'Mr Staples, do you agree that dynamic, expanding businesses like yours need up to the minute information at very short notice?'
'Of course, it is essential.'
'Well, Mr. Staples, providing up to the minute systems is our business. . .'

'Good morning, Ms Lightfoot, would you agree that your shelf space is highly valuable to you?'
The retailer, Ms Lightfoot, must answer, 'Yes.'
'If', the salesman then continues, 'you could display the same products and still have 20 per cent space available for other goods, you would think it worth while, wouldn't you?'
'Yes.'
'Our new lamps are 20 per cent smaller than those we

used to make, but they have the same output and last just as long. You will not only find them quick-moving, but as they take up so much less space on your shelves, you will have more room to display more goods. I am from. . .'

'Good morning, Mr Hawkins, can you sell high-quality power drills in your shop?'

This question prompts two thoughts in the mind of the prospect: firstly, 'This fellow doesn't think I can sell high-quality products! I'll show him I can'; secondly, 'He must be very certain of the quality of his products to ask me such a question!'

When he answers, 'Yes', the salesman continues, 'Then, sir, I can show you how you can make extra profits by selling the most expensive but finest quality drill on the market. I am from. . .'

'Good morning, Dr Alexander. Isn't it true, doctor, that more and more patients visit your surgery suffering from migraine?'

'Yes, it's a growing twentieth-century complaint.'

'Well, doctor, my company, XYZ Ltd, has developed a new treatment about which an article appeared in the *Lancet* recently, and I should like to amplify one or two of the points made in it. . .'

'Good morning, Mr Giles. Would you agree that one of the biggest overheads in farming today is that of labour costs?'

'Yes, I suppose so.'

'Well, sir, my company, Better Fertilisers Ltd, has produced a new fertiliser which is so concentrated that much less labour is needed to spread it; but it is more effective than the normal type of fertiliser because. . .'

'Good morning Mrs Gardener. Do you agree that your job as a retailer is made much easier by manufacturers who go all out to stimulate public demand for their products?'

'Yes, that is so.'

'My company, Tissues Ltd, conducts the biggest advertising campaign in the trade, and I should like to give you details of our new programme for the next three months. . .'

'Good morning, Miss Goldberg. Isn't it your experience that a very large proportion of men's toiletries are purchased by women?'

'Yes, that's true.'

'It is because of this that my company, XYZ Ltd, has designed its products for men with women in mind. Let me show you an example of the new type of pack we have produced. . .'

There is of course a similarity between stating a fact and asking a question. A fact can be turned into a question, in the same way as many questions can be turned into facts, but there is one difference in these openings. With the question opening the salesman expects, and receives, a reply. With the factual opening he states the fact, arouses the buyer's interest, but doesn't pause for an answer. He continues with his sales offer.

The reference opening

What is the ideal attention-getting technique? If used properly, it is the reference opening.

Let us think again of what immediately interests us. When considering a holiday in some sun-baked Mediterranean resort, we cannot make up our mind which of the hotels in the package deal to choose. Then a friend says to us, 'You must stay at the Capitol Hotel – it's absolutely marvellous. The food's wonderful, and the

service couldn't be bettered. Do you know they
even...'

Do we hesitate? Not for one moment! We immediately book at the Capitol, and tell everyone we meet
that we are going to stay at a highly recommended
hotel.

If we need dental treatment a friend may say, 'You
ought to go to Mr Sinclair in the High Street; he's the
most wonderful dentist I've ever known. He hates to
cause you pain. You know how nervous I always am...'
And off we go to meet Mr Sinclair.

What do we do when a business acquaintance says,
'Why don't you go and see Mr Lane of Kerr Brothers, it
seems just right for him. He's a friend of mine –
mention my name.'

Very quickly we telephone Mr Lane for an appointment and Mr Lane will undoubtedly see us, because he
knows that his friend wouldn't waste his time. The
mind of a buyer is always influenced by a recommenda-
tion from someone he knows.

It can also be influenced if he is shown, very early in
the interview, a letter stressing the benefits of your
products, written by an executive of a reputable company. But never use a letter written by the buyer's
competitor – that can antagonise him. In addition, be
very careful about showing a letter from a giant organisation to the managing director employing some fifty
people. His response could then be, 'It's all right for
them with their millions, but we aren't big enough'.

The sales-aid opening

What is it that makes husbands put down their newspapers, or tycoons turn away from important matters?
Curiosity! When a buyer sees a salesman unwrapping a
small parcel, or opening a case in which something is
gleaming brightly, or taking a plastic container out of

his pocket, that buyer won't want the salesman to leave before he finds out what it is that gleams in the leather case, what new concept is in the plastic container, what is so special about that parcel. . . The sales-aid opening, being based on the natural curiosity of most people, will always get a buyer's undivided attention.

If, by using a sales aid, you can cover all the prospect's five senses – sight, touch, taste, smell, and hearing – you will make a very good opening. This can rarely be achieved, but the objective should be to appeal to as many of the senses as possible as quickly as possible.

Catalogues, descriptions or specifications of equipment, photographs of installations, independent test reports, performance graphs, reproductions of testimonial letters from well-known companies . . . can all be used as sales-aid openers. Salesmen selling to retailers and wholesalers will have samples of their range, especially new products, which obviously they will show.

At the opening you do not want the buyer to read through a brochure line by line – he would only pretend to do so, anyway. When using literature as a sales-aid opener, the salesman must pinpoint one particular feature applicable to the buyer's business. The salesman should always maintain control of the interview by holding the leaflet up and pointing out the features. He should not hand it over for the buyer to study, thus enabling him to glance casually at each page, which half-hearted interest could lead him to decide that he is not interested.

The sales-aid opening can be most effective if linked with a factual, or question opening.

The demonstration opening

Pen and paper can provide an excellent demonstration opening, which can immediately interest the buyer in the sales offer.

A salesman's opening sentence could be: 'We can move ten of your crates in ten minutes. This will mean a saving in time of...' The salesman then continues, writing down the total number of crates handled in a week, and begins working out the saving in time. Then on to cost reduction, continually bringing the buyer in the calculations.

If, however, you are able to demonstrate equipment, the buyer will quickly pay attention, so that there is very little need for attention-getting sentences.

When you demonstrate at the opening of a sale, remember these points:

1 Never demonstrate with an imperfect unit.
2 Whenever possible, let the buyer sell himself on the unit by allowing him to work the model.
3 Always demonstrate very slowly. Make sure that your prospect is following each point, by asking him questions.

Sometimes it is better to list features/benefits of a unit before the demonstration takes place. On other occasions, however, a demonstration opening can be most effective, with each benefit being stressed as the demonstration progresses.

Calling back

There are many reasons for industrial salesmen to call back on prospective buyers or customers, other than that of obtaining an order. Such objectives can be termed *development calls*. At every contact, high or low, the salesman must attempt to develop the worth and profitability of the relationship.

Here are some examples:

1 To negotiate long-term business.
2 To get products or services specified.

3   To get repeat orders.
4   To continue negotiations.
5   To carry out a survey.
6   To handle a complaint.
7   To discover the real reason why a competitor is obtaining business – buyers rarely give the real reason for changing.
8   To maintain goodwill by showing operators how to get the best out of equipment sold.
9   To get an introduction to another buyer.
10 To make certain that assistants know all the benefits of products, and the full range of your company's services.
11 To gain knowledge of production conditions.
12 To get agreement to visit a factory, or stage a demonstration of equipment.
13 To establish needs.
14 To get agreement from a production manager to allow a visit to his works by a prospective customer.
15 To present quotations, specifications, costings, changes in schedule.

Let us consider three of these objectives, and how they can be tackled by salesmen.

1   *To maintain goodwill, and keep out competition, by showing machine operators – or any other employees – how to get the best out of the equipment sold*
Does the salesman approach the machine operators (having first, of course, obtained the necessary permission) and say, 'I know you're all a bit thick, so I thought I'd call to show you how to obtain the best results from this equipment. . .' or 'It hardly seems possible but even now some of you don't know the full capabilities of this equipment'. You can imagine what would be the results if a salesman were to use such an opening. He must therefore take great care to plan in advance exactly what he is going to say, in order to ensure that there is

no risk of antagonising anyone. His objective is to make sure that all the operators are well sold on the equipment, so that when new orders are placed, they will speak highly of it.

The salesman can use any of the standard openings – asking a question, or stating a fact:

(a) 'Do any of you find any difficulty in using the threaded. . .?'
(b) 'I have found on some calls that operators have not been told initially that by using the barlock at No. 10 frequency, there is no risk of. . .'

In neither of these openings does he risk upsetting the operators, and he is using exactly the same *form* of opening as he would if his objective was to sell the equipment, instead of calling back to maintain goodwill and increase product knowledge.

2   *To get an introduction to another buyer*
In exactly the same way as if he were selling, the salesman would plan how to phrase the opening sentence. He might ask a question:

> 'Mr Pizey, do you know if Mr Kenton in your S Division uses block struts, as you do here?'
> 'I'm not certain.'
> 'Then would you mind introducing me to him, so that I can see if we may be helpful to his division, as we always try to be to yours?'

3   *To discover the real reason why a competitor is obtaining business – buyers rarely give the real reason*
To achieve this objective can be difficult. Should it be achieved by trying to wheedle the information out of an employee? Surely this form of ferreting out information borders on the unethical.

The salesman might therefore decide to use a

fact-plus question opening, while talking to a friendly employee:

> 'John, as you know, we supply over 60 percent of the Cyclatones in the British Isles – and that percentage increases every year – but we still don't want to lose any of it. Can you tell me, therefore, if there is any reason why Mr Preston, your buyer, has decided to use Cyclatones supplied by XYZ?'

Most people react to a direct question, and John will probably be no different from anyone else.

Although the objectives of a salesman may be varied, and may cover a wide area, the majority call to negotiate or obtain orders. Sometimes a salesman may call on a buyer twenty times or more, in an attempt to open the account. Salesmen supplying customers with component parts may call every four weeks on a buyer; others may call only twice or three times a year; *but* following the *chat gap* the salesman must still obtain the undivided attention of the buyer, assistant buyer, research and development manager, accountant . . . whoever it is whose mind the salesman has to influence.

Every salesman at every call must have an objective, and on that objective will be based the opening technique he uses. Without an objective a salesman risks using a colourless, cliché-ridden opening, which makes it easy for the buyer to end the interview quickly.

As much care must be taken with the call-back opening as with a first call. All the standard techniques may be used, when calling back.

Here are some examples.

Factual openings

'Because of the world shortage of Salycotes we shall shortly be changing to a synthetic. I felt sure you would want to place a large order now, while the Salycotes are still available. . .'

'Mr Edwards, you are using approximately 120,000 metres of Dylet a month. An analysis of your orders over the past three years shows a steady growth, which means that within three months you will be needing 150,000 metres regularly. Deliveries are getting tighter, and I don't want to let you down, so if you order now. . .'

Both of these openings can lead to a quick close.

Question openings

'The trend seems to be to switch from transistors to monitors. How is that going to affect your production lines?'
    'It could cause problems.'
    'Well, here's a way that we can help you. . .'

'How does the labour shortage in this area affect you, Miss Montgomery?'
    'It's getting worse every day.'
    'There is a way we can help you: since I last called we have devised a pre-pack which will save you. . .'

Reference opening

'Mr Griffiths, I called on your friend Brian Walker yesterday. He suggested that I should tell you about the results he is getting with Gripit. You haven't used it for some time now, Mr Griffiths, but I'm sure you will want to consider it again. . .'

Sales-aid opening

'I've brought you our latest catalogue, Mrs Lyons. It gives a complete range of spare parts now – which is in line with the suggestion you made a year ago. I'd like to show you. . .'

When a salesman calls regularly on retail/wholesale customers, he should dispense with such stock phrases as:

'How are you?'
'Has the stock been moving?'
'Is trade any better?'
'Were the goods delivered on time?'
'Did the display arrive?'
'Anything for me today?'

These are time-wasters. No matter how frequently a salesman sees a customer, he can find something new to say about his products. Before each visit he should decide on a factual sentence, a question, or a term of reference, that will put fresh life into the sale. For example:

1 'Good morning, Mr Mills. When I was here last month I told you about our new advertising campaign. I have some facts for you now which should help you to decide on your stock requirements.'
2 'Good morning, Mrs Reed. Have you noticed that over the past five weeks there has been a sudden demand for reds and greens? We have added some variations of these colours to our range. . .'
3 'Mr Chadwick, after I left you last time I thought of an idea which would help you to sell more of. . .'
4 'Good morning Miss Green, I must apologise to you. When I was here five weeks ago I didn't really explain in detail what a tie-up with our promotional campaign means. But you will remember that you were very busy at the time. Do forgive me; this is how it can help you. . .'

The professional salesman thinks of something new at every call. Most salesmen use the factual, question, or reference approach. The following additional forms of approach can, however, be used occasionally.

The curiosity approach

'Good morning, Miss Birch. Have you ever seen a metal plate like this before? It can save you a lot of money; it is an accessory used in our new addressing machine...'

The fear approach

'Mr Webber, what would happen to your house if a fire broke out while you and your children were asleep in bed? Our new alarm...'

The gift approach

'Mrs Taylor? Good morning. Will you please accept this cleaning powder with our compliments? We want you to try it, and I also want to show you...'

The personal interest approach

'Good morning, Mr Parsons. I was very interested to read your excellent letter in this morning's *Telegraph*. Every statement you made was quite right, but naturally I was sorry to hear of the bad service you had received from the X Car Company. This need never happen to you again. I am from the ABC Garage. We are sole distributors in the area for Y cars, and I have called to ask you to allow us to show you a model of...'

The link opening

Have you seen any TV thriller serials lately? If so, you will have noticed the regular use of the technique of showing a flashback from the final scene of the previous episode. It is this link with the past which immediately arouses the viewer's interest in the new episode.

The link opening in selling uses the same technique as the flashback on TV. A point discussed at one call becomes the link to hold the buyer's attention at the beginning of the next call.

Although the link technique can be used whatever the objective of the call-back, it is most useful to those industrial salesmen whose products are repeatable and who therefore call on their buyers every four to six weeks, year in and year out. 'What can I say that's new', they ask, 'when we have nothing exciting to offer for periods of six or nine months, or more?'

To those salesmen, the link helps to maintain a continuing dialogue, the salesman probing, questioning, reminding . . . with the objective of selling strongly at every call to get the maximum business *at every call*. Sometimes only a few words are needed, words most pleasing to a buyer: 'You will remember when last I called you said. . .' We are all always ready to hear our own words of wisdom repeated.

If this link is not feasible, the salesman can refer to a question left unanswered, a statement made by a third party, or a point made previously, in which the buyer has shewn interest. For example:

1   'Mr Armstrong, you will remember last month you said that the problem of off-cuts was becoming acute. I have been thinking very deeply about this point, and I want to suggest that. .'

2   'Mr Savage, when I was here last week you told me of your plans to. . . This is how we can help your plans along. . .'

3   'Mrs White, when I brought in your quotation last week, I shewed you the drawings, but I forgot to mention. . .'

There is one DON'T that every salesman should remember when working out a link opening.

If, at a previous call, you have dealt with a complaint and settled it, *DON'T* bring the matter up again by saying, 'Is the machine working all right now?' This will begin a trend of negative thoughts in the buyer's mind. If anything is wrong, he will soon tell you.

Always recall *positive* points:

(a) 'Mr Jarvis, last month you told me that it was essential for you to have the motors by the 24th. Well, they left for the site yesterday, the 17th. As I promised, I was determined to give your order priority – but, Mr Jarvis, deliveries will get progressively worse, and I feel sure that you will now want to. . .'

(b) 'I really appreciated the confidence you showed in me when I called last month and you told me of what was happening. Well, Mrs Black, *The Times* only published the news yesterday, but those three weeks have enabled us to draw up a new plan for you. . .'

(c) 'There was one point we touched on last week, Mr Lucas, when I called, and that was the noise factor. You said you were going to look into the question and of course with embossing machines the noise can sometimes be deafening. Now with our machines there is less noise than that of a typewriter. . .'

(d) 'Mr Bright, when I was here last week, I promised to bring you a photograph of some of our non-ferrous castings, to give you some indication of how our experience can help you. I have had this photograph taken specially for you. . .'

Getting attention

1   Never sell under adverse conditions.

2 Don't gabble; always speak slowly so that the buyer
   can hear every word.
3 Keep the *chat gap* as short as possible.
4 Make certain that you have worked out the best
   possible opening sentence.
5 When calling back, make sure that you get attention
   by using any of the standard openings, or a link
   opening.
6 Always remember the objective of the opening is to
   obtain the undivided attention of the buyer.

Work out a new approach which will hold attention
with your very first few words. It can be done – and
YOU can do it!

9 The winning close

Our first open sales-training course consisted of fifteen delegates. Three were from companies that had contacted us following the publicity mentioned earlier, and the remaining twelve were from companies called on by my brother or me. Among them were delegates from British European Airways (one of the forerunners of British Airways), Brown & Polson (then leaders in fast-moving consumer goods, since taken over), Norwich Union, Eversheds (leading printers then, as they are today), Lansing Bagnall (fork-lift trucks), Glaxo, Paton & Baldwin, and Spicers. Forty years on these companies are still using our training services.

The course room was an office converted for the occasion, and our delegates had to sit for three days on hard kitchen chairs which we had picked up at a sale. Bench tables were made up for us by our handyman and maintenance engineer, Bert Hanks. It was an era of shortages, following the war. We had no visual aids, there was very little participation, no films – a style which would not succeed these days, and rightly so! But much of our success then was due to our certainty that we were right about everything relating to salesmanship. We believed it was our duty so to inspire others about the righteousness of our cause that success would be achieved automatically, by all the delegates. Turnover would definitely increase, with repeat business following.

At the opening of that first course, and those to follow for some years, I said, 'Your company has paid a large fee (£12!) to send you here. There is only one reason for their decision: so that, beginning next Monday, your sales will increase substantially. They would not want us to teach you "ifs" and "buts", "maybes" or "perhapses", or even "possiblys". They want us to tell you exactly what you have to do to put 10 per cent, 20 per cent, 30 per cent on your turnover.

'We respect their views. You have not come here for discussions, you have come to learn how we train salesmen to succeed, knowing that our teachings are based on research in depth, and the practices in the field of our own large salesforce. We experiment with them, not with you. Therefore, gentlemen (no "ladies" in those days!), we pledge that we shall not sit on any fences. You may well disagree with our advice on occasion, but still do as we say. Try it, to prove to yourselves which of us is right. If we are wrong, you will report this back to your company, and no more delegates will arrive here from them – that's for sure! But if you do carry out the precepts we teach, then I guarantee you success.'

The repeat business we obtained in those days proved that although the courses then did not compare with those of the present day, which are mainly participative, and of course include films, videos, computers, workshops, etc., enthusiastic and inspirational teaching had its value then, as it has today.

Our success still relies on the ability of our instructors to inspire delegates to carry out our teachings. Lukewarm delegates may have a mine of information stored away in their heads, but it will remain there unless it is activated by inspiration and enthusiasm. My objective in this book is to encourage you to carry out the techniques outlined; otherwise, you may well say to yourself, 'All good stuff, but it doesn't apply to me'.

Often a managing director, sales director, or sales manager, will visit us and say something like this: 'You inspired me. You told me exactly what I had to do. I did it – maybe others didn't'.

As salesmen you must never sit on a fence. You must be definite in your views, in statements. To repeat once more: *the only way a salesman can show strength is by the words he uses* – not by shouting, not by looking aggressive, not by thumping desks, but only by the use of words. During the sales presentation you must use your words and expressions to motivate and show your strength, so that the nudge towards the end will enable you to make many more closes.

No gimmicks

In those early days, in the USA, which we visited regularly, there were many advertised courses extolling the virtues of the magic close, the pick-up-the-hat close, the low pressure/high pressure close... These are the ones I remember. There were others, even more suggestive of some unusual, spectacular way of closing more orders.

When looking at such courses, or reading books written on these subjects, one saw that they were only using the standard closing techniques but dressing them up in inspirational jargon. Even today salesmen are looking for some magic close – but magic closes don't exist!

However, perhaps I am being too dogmatic. There is one form of closing which is almost akin to magic, because it works so often.

The only sure way to close more orders

If you are asked on a television or radio show to name a world-wide Channel-swimming star, you might well answer, 'Captain Webb, who was the first to swim the Channel in 1875'. But if I had been asked that question as a youthful swimming enthusiast, I should have answered, 'Temme'. Temme broke the cross-Channel record, and then broke it again. He was the hero of our time.

One day Temme and his entourage, including myself, were awaiting the return of yet another attempted Channel crossing by a swimmer. The first we became aware that the swimmer was nearly home was when we saw the small accompanying boats containing the umpire, trainers, and well-wishers. Then a few hundred yards out we saw the swimmer being helped on to a boat. Later we learned that he had been taken ill and become too exhausted to continue.

Someone said to Temme, 'What a shame to fail by those few yards, after swimming all those miles'.

Temme replied, 'He didn't fail because the crossing was a few yards too long, he failed a long way back. He may have chosen the wrong strategy, he may not have anticipated the weather or tides correctly, his training could have been too hard or too soft, he could have used the wrong combination of swimming strokes. . .'

Although these were not the exact words that Temme used, his meaning was clear.

We told that Temme story at our courses for many years. The lesson is so simple. A good presentation leads to many more sales being closed. Orders are not lost at the last minute, any more than that swimmer lost at the final stage. Sales are nearly always lost during the preparation or the presentation.

Many salesmen have said to me, 'I was doing well until the close' or 'I had the order in the bag, I was almost counting up my commission, when I was put off'. My response to them is generally, 'You were not all right until the close, you never had the order in the bag. What you now have to do is to check up on your presentation'.

Boris Becker, on losing the Masters' Tennis final in New York said, 'It's back to basics for me!'

Remember Becker. Remember Temme.

If you are not closing enough orders, go back to basics. (Sorry to have to keep repeating this so often, but your success can depend on your constantly returning to basics.) Search through your presentation for weaknesses. Check on all the benefits, carry out offer analysis, in case you have missed a benefit.

Do that, and the only technique you will need at the end of the presentation is a *nudge* sentence.

There are no great closing techniques, no brilliant concepts for nailing down the buyer. Only good salesmanship closes the maximum number of orders, and that is simply a matter of good presentation.

Before we consider the various nudges, there are some other benefits concerned with closing the sale.

The myth of the psychological moment

The myth of the psychological moment for closing the order, like the myth of the born salesman, continues. There is no one psychological closing moment, for if the order is lost, it is certainly lost during the presentation. There are times when, because of buying signals, a salesman is aware that an opportune moment for closing has arisen, but you can forget the psychological moment. Aside from the buying signals, the only time to close is when you are certain that the buyer fully understands your proposal, has heard all the evidence, and is then mentally attuned to making a decision.

A 'yes' response is a buying signal. Obviously if you don't get the correct response, not only will you have to settle any doubts in his mind, but you will also have to reassess your presentation, because you have disclosed a weakness which you must correct.

Here are some questions which should obtain the 'yes' response, or enable the salesman to reassess the position or reinforce the arguments he is putting forward:

1 'Mr Sharples, you do agree that the fitness centre will appeal to those attending your conference here?'
2 'Mr Logan, you do need the terminals to be precisely controlled, don't you?'
3 'Mr Wright, do you agree that you need a tailor-made financial solution to enable you to carry out your future plans?'
4 'Mrs Morrison, it will take a load off your mind, won't it, when you know that you have the backing of our worthwhile network.'
5 'Mr Hopkins, you will admit that the thermostat cut-out will save money, won't it?'
6 'Miss Ingram, don't you think it is just the right time now to join us in our promotion?'
7 'Mr Harris, it would be a most attractive window display – I'm sure you'll agree that passers-by will stop to look at it, won't they?'
8 'Mr Dennis, this is the design you had in mind, isn't it?'
9 'Mr Lincoln, it's a fast moving line, and that's what you want, isn't it?'
10 'Miss Fletcher, these new designs are attractive, aren't they?'

There are of course exceptions, when hardly any 'yes' responses are required. A buyer telephones you to call because he needs a product urgently and has made up his mind in advance of your call; a buyer knows that, owing to shortages, he must stock up quickly; or perhaps there is shortly going to be a price rise. In these situations you must close the order as quickly as possible, to save your time as well as that of the buyer.

Promises – promises. . .

If you are easily misled by buyers, you will find difficulty in closing orders. We all have techniques we use when we don't want to make a decision. 'I'll have to ask my wife (husband, partner, boss, committee. . .) about it.' It may be true, it may be false, but you should always assume that it is false, because it usually is.

Another get-out for the indecisive buyer is to ask you to leave him a leaflet. He might then say something like this, 'It's all procedure, of course – it doesn't mean anything – but I must show it to Mr Basil, and clear it with the financial director. They never say no to my requests, but I have to go through the normal channels. Give me a ring in about two weeks' time.'

'Thank you' is the salesman's response, when mentally he should be thinking, 'Not much chance of an order here!'.

I have no statistics to work on, but I'm sure I would not be far out by suggesting that 70 per cent of such promises are used as an excuse to get rid of the salesman – not necessarily because the proposal is bad but simply because the buyer, although 90 per cent convinced that he needs your product or service, doesn't have to make an urgent decision and would rather procrastinate. Alternatively, he may be the weak kind of buyer who doesn't want to hurt your feelings, or doesn't want to get into an argument at that time, realising that most salesmen will persevere. With some buyers, procrastination has just become a habit.

Whatever the reason, the salesman should recognise the buying put-off technique and, while apparently agreeing to return later or leave a leaflet, etc., will go back to square one and start selling all over again. He may then discover the real reason why the buyer doesn't want to say 'Yes'. For example, the salesman may not have been using the 'Yes' response technique throughout the sale, and therefore planted doubts in the buyer's mind.

The salesmen employed in the various divisions of our organisation know that they must never tell me about 'that certain prospect'. In this building we never listen to such words as 'the order's in the bag', 'this will be a definite sale next week', 'it's only waiting for the signature, and that's held up because Mr So-and-So is away'.

My response is, 'Only signed orders get me excited. Tell me again why there is a delay. . .'

Everyone at Tack is tired of me telling the story of the seven noes, but perhaps you will hear it now for the first time!

During an era of economic decline one salesman in an organisation continued to produce record results. He gave no indication of how this success was achieved, not through any selfishness on his part but because he was not conscious that he was exceptional. One day his sales manager decided to join this star salesman on his travels.

At each call he noticed that the salesman transferred an object from one pocket to another. After watching him do this on several calls, the sales manager said to him, 'Now I know the reason for your success. You succeed because you are so persevering. Nothing puts you off. Back you go, time and time again, to one of the benefits. But you seem to be taking something out of one pocket and transferring it to another all the time. Is that some superstitious rite?'

'Oh no', said the salesman. 'It's my plan for making sure that I never give up until I have received seven noes.'

The manager looked puzzled, and the salesman continued, I keep seven coins in my right-hand jacket pocket. The first time the buyer says no, I transfer one of the coins to another pocket, and I repeat this when I get the second no, and so on. Only if and when all seven coins have changed pockets without my succeeding, do I pick up my bag and leave – but I never, never leave until after I have received seven noes. That way, I'm sure of not giving up too soon.'

That's right! Too many salesmen give up too soon.

The sales-aid close

It was a hot night, and the humidity seemed to be about 100 per cent. All around me were men and women perspiring freely, and the conditions were anything but right for a pleasant evening – and yet we did have a pleasant evening.

It was 1948 and we were watching Joe Louis defend his world heavyweight title against Jersey Joe Walcott. There wasn't much excitement to start with; the men looked like two black marble statues after a cleaner had poured water over them, and the lighting above the ring reflected from their shining bodies.

Louis shuffled after Walcott, hardly hitting at all, but moving forward all the time. Walcott boxed on the retreat, but kept slipping under Louis' arms and scoring with his left. Louis hardly used his right at all – he kept it back for the pay-off. And the pay-off came unexpectedly. That right came across, and when it landed, we all knew that Walcott wouldn't recover – and he didn't. Joe Louis never wasted his right – *he kept it back for use at the right moment.*

Too many salesmen waste their best punches early in the sales battle. Because they are armed with a host of sales aids and a string of verbal proof stories, they feel it is their duty to show everything and tell everything as quickly as possible. They haven't the time to show pride of ownership in their leaflets – they produce them so quickly that any startling effect that they should have on the prospect is lost.

This is brought about by the salesman's anxiety to impress quickly, and to overwhelm the prospect with his sales aids and talk. Enthusiastic selling is always good, provided the salesman knows what he is doing and is not just losing his head. The element of surprise is as important in a sale as it is in a fight.

Most salesmen have one particular sales aid which they prefer to all others. All salesmen have one story which they like to tell, because it always gets a good reaction. Now here is my advice to you: *Retain in your bag whatever you consider to be your best sales aid until the sale is at least three-quarters of the way through,* and at the same time *keep your best story for use as a closing aid.*

Now take time off to think about this, and when you have decided on your sales aid, put it aside, and keep it back as long as you can. Every time you are tempted to use it during a sale, wait a little longer.

This will result in your sales story being better, because you are building it, to start off with, around your weaker tools. It means that you will have to rely more on your sales ability. Then, when you bring out your best ammunition, you will find closing the order will become much easier for you.

The rule for every salesman to remember is to *use his second-best sales aid for the approach, and his best sales aid for the close.*

Ask

You have completed your sales offer and believe that you have interpreted a buying signal correctly. What can happen?

1 The buyer says, 'Right, I'll have it!' or words to that effect.
2 The buyer still hesitates, waiting for you to prompt

him for a decision. If you, too, hesitate, he will
regain his authority and say, 'Call again towards the
end of next week. By then I shall have had a chance
to (speak to someone, see someone, think it
over...)'.

3 You ask for the order.

The average salesman is afraid to ask for a decision.
He would rather create a prospect than risk losing the
order. He is quite happy to be told to come back next
week. There has been no victory, but neither has there
been any defeat.

This fear of asking for the order must be overcome if
a salesman is to succeed. Every buyer knows why
salesmen are employed and why they make calls – they
want orders. Yet possibly as many as 30 per cent of all
orders are lost because the salesman is afraid to ask the
direct question, 'May I have the order?'

It need not always be as direct as this, but if it is, very
few buyers will object.

The salesman may prefer to say:

(a) 'You can always telephone me regarding after-sales
    service. Now let me note down the details...'
(b) 'I'll telephone the office straight away, to have four
    units put aside for you...'
(c) 'I'm sure it will, Mr Congreve, so shall we get the
    details settled?...'
(d) 'You'll want it then, Miss Sheridan. If you will give
    me an order number straight away, I can start
    getting the order processed...'
(e) 'I'll write the order up, Mr Hope...'

If every salesman made up his mind to ask for the order
at every opportunity (that is, of course, whenever a
buyer is able to give a decision), he would break every
target set by his sales manager.

Closing techniques

There are many occasions when a hesitant buyer needs
a 'nudge' before he will make up his mind, even after
he has given buying signals. There are closing techniques which do enable a salesman to urge the buyer
gently towards making his decision.

The alternative close

If a prospective buyer is hesitant and doesn't give a
clear buying signal, there is a risk in asking directly for
the order. He could say 'Yes', but he could also say
'No!', and the salesman is then faced with the difficult
task of persuading him to change his mind. By offering
the buyer alternatives the salesman is not inviting a
'Yes' or 'No', he is only asking the buyer to tell him
which of the alternatives he prefers.

It is true he could answer 'Neither', but remember
we are now dealing with the hesitant buyer, not the one
who has strong objections to buying. This buyer, who
wants to buy but can't make up his mind, only requires
very gentle persuasion to help him arrive at a final
decision.

Here are some examples ot the alternative close:

1   'The unit can be installed in that corner, or close to
    the sorting machine. Which do you prefer?'
2   'Would you prefer our cleaners to work early in the
    mornings or after hours in the evenings?'
3   'Do you prefer the finish in grey or black?'
4   'Do you want us to hold, pending instructions, or
    deliver to the site?'
5   'Do you want us to deliver the truck or would you
    prefer to collect it from our depot?'
6   'Do you want a solid fixing or would you rather the
    unit was easily movable?'

7 'Do you require the extra long extension or would our standard ten-foot extension suit you?'
8 'Will you take eight gross or ten?'
9 'Will you take advantage of our discount for twelve issues or would you prefer to test the response by advertising in six issues to begin with?'

When the buyer states his preference, the salesman should accept his answer as denoting a willingness to buy, and should begin to note down details, or ask for the order number.

The summary close

Have you a good memory? If so, you are very fortunate. Many people can't remember what they said two minutes earlier, let alone what someone else told them. Most of us would be hard put to remember everything we were told during a recent conversation. That is why defence and prosecuting counsels and the judge summarise for the jury – to remind them of all the facts of the case.

At the end of the sales offer the buyer may have forgotten an important benefit, so the salesman must remind him of the main benefits he has outlined during the sale. For example:

1 'Mrs Gregory, there are so many benefits that our Chromart will give you. You will save your present dual costing system, because it is a combined electronic calculator and typewriter. Secondly, invoices can be typed, additions made on the same machine, and discounts printed. Thirdly, you will cut direct costs because, when set at automatic, you can produce statements from sets of invoices. And fourthly, it will save you space, because it is smaller than a standard electric typewriter. . .'

2 'Mr Young, I should like to sum up for you all the
   many advantages of Apex Automated Lathes. One,
   the Apex will handle parallel and taper turning,
   drilling, and knurling. Two, it will handle your
   continuous operations, including of course internal
   and external threading. Three, a sophisticated prog-
   rammer controls the hydraulically operated Apex.
   Four, a programme allows for six cross-slide and
   eight tailstock operations. Five, your operator will
   be able to depend on a control panel which shows
   the cycle currently in operation. Mr Young, I have
   stressed to you the benefits you will derive from
   each of these five features, but there is an additional
   one, which is that the Apex will cost you no more
   than any machine without these refinements. It only
   needs a power point. Perhaps you would like to
   show me which one will be most convenient for
   you. . .'

The salesman would not list every benefit – that would
be too time-consuming – and because he has already
stated the benefits, he can, as in the example of the
Apex Automated Lathe, restate only the main features
and then turn them into a final benefit. On completion,
the salesman should always ask direct for the order or
offer alternatives.

The fear close

The fear close must be used sparingly. Many buyers
react to it unfavourably. It can be effective for salesmen
of goods in short supply, or insurance, fire-exting-
uishers, burglar alarms, or other safety devices:

(a) 'You will want me to give you cover right away,
    Mrs Callaghan. After all, if someone dropped a
    lighted match in a waste-paper basket this after-

noon and caused a fire, you would bear the loss.
When I have your agreement to this policy, we
bear the loss. . .'
(b) 'Mr Butler, as you know, the new Act could mean
heavy fines if office conditions were unsatisfactory.
You are too good a businessman to take that risk.
I'll see that you get delivery quickly.'
(c) 'With the season approaching, our delivery will
extend to about six weeks. This won't be of any use to
you. Be on the safe side and place your order now, or
competitors will be carrying stocks before you.'

Estate agents probably use this close more than
others. They often have a waiting list for a house, and
can honestly say, 'I'm afraid you must make up your
mind quickly, as there are two or three other people
after it'.

Verbal-proof story close

Earlier in the sale you may have told your prospect of
other satisfied users of your equipment or service. But
always try to save one verbal-proof story for the close.
  You might conclude like this:

When I first called on Mr Smith of Smith & White, he
was very dubious that our products would sell in his
shop. His shop is at Kenton, as you know, and very
much like your own. He serves the same kind of
people and stocks similar goods. I found it hard to
convince him then that he would succeed with our
merchandise, but he is a man of decision – like you –
and he placed a trial order. Now this is one of his best
selling lines, and it can be the same in your shop. . .'

Keep back a good story for the close; one that will
swing the prospect in your favour.

The isolation close

One main reason usually prevents a prospect from buying, and the salesman must isolate it, in order to answer it. He asks the prospect for any such reasons, and writes them down:

'Let me be perfectly clear about what you want, Mr Gilbert', he should say, and then begin to write:

'One, you don't like the standard finish.

'Two, you can't wait three months for delivery.

'Three, you want three months' credit from the date of installation. Is that so, Mr Gilbert?'

Mr Gilbert agrees, and then the salesman takes each point and shows how it can be overcome. At last, he isolates the main reason why the prospect doesn't want to sign the order. This may be the lack of three months' credit terms.

'All that separates us, then, Mr Gilbert, is that you need extended credit facilities. Let me telephone our accounts department now, and I can get it settled right away.'

'Influencing the mind' close

Salesmen of certain products cannot close an order. For instance, ethical pharmaceuticals are advertised only in medical journals, and can be supplied only through prescription. The doctor doesn't buy them, and the chemist does so only when he receives a prescription for the drug. Although the salesman cannot close the order, he must so influence the mind of the doctor that he will prescribe his drugs.

Again he obtains 'Yes' responses, and may say, at the end of the sales presentation: 'You will probably think it a good idea if I call on Badcock's the chemists, and tell them to be sure to have stocks available. . .', or 'You will find this drug so helpful that I am sure you will prescribe it over and over again, so I had better call at the chemist and advise him. . .'

The sale cannot be closed, but the doctor's mind can be influenced. That, after all, is the same as a close.

Closing on a minor point

This is a form of trial close. The salesman has lost little if the minor point is not acceptable to the buyer. He can continue with his sales offer and try to close again later.

Here are some examples of *closing on a minor point*:

1 'You do prefer the anti-corrosive finish, don't you, Mr Lock?'
2 'Would you like me to bring you those drawings to-morrow morning?'
3 'Shall I arrange for an engineer to telephone you in the morning to discuss installation?'
4 'Don't you think it would be a change for the better, Ms Prior, if the print on the carton could be changed from blue to red?'
5 'Do you like the idea of the pilot light being combined with the buzzer?'
6 'You'll need three showcards, won't you?'
7 'You'll find our new display stand really does move the stock. You will of course want. . .'

When the buyer agrees on the minor point, the salesman again accepts that the order is his, notes down details, or offers alternatives.

The concession close

There are occasions when a salesman is allowed to make a special concession to customers. This may be a standard quantity discount for orders of fifty units or more, and as a special concession the salesman might be allowed to offer the discount for only forty units; a guarantee could be extended from one year to two, as a boost for sales; trade-in allowances could be increased; a survey for which a charge is usually made could be offered free; or there could be a special concession of a free supply of refills for machines. Other forms of concession could be a willingness to hold stocks, to be drawn upon as required; a guarantee to hold prices for six months; or free delivery to site.

When a salesman is allowed to make a special concession he usually uses it in his opening: 'Mr Bull, you will be pleased to hear that for orders of 300 units placed now we will extend credit for six months, without charging any interest. . .'

Why should that please Mr Bull when, possibly, he doesn't know at that stage whether he will need to place so large an order, nor whether he can use up the supply within the six-month period? If he can buy at a similar price elsewhere and pay monthly for the goods, he may still be better off than placing an order for 300.

Until the buyer is persuaded that all the benefits offered, when added up, will make the purchase worth while for him, he may not be deeply interested in a special concession. Even if a regular supplier offers a special concession, the buyer may try to get the concession without meeting the special demands of the supplier (taking immediate delivery or a larger quantity, or stocking a new range of components). It is much wiser therefore to hold back the concession and use it to help close the order. Then, when the buyer is mentally weighing up the pros and cons of the offer, and perhaps benefits and costs stay equally poised, the salesman may tip the scales in his favour in the following ways:

(a) 'Mrs Slater, I'm sure that the range of adhesives will be of immense value to you, but as an extra incentive for you to buy now, I can give you. . .'

(b) 'Our normal delivery is about eight weeks, sir, but I know you will benefit so much from the equipment when it is installed that I am going to put pressure on the works to make a concession in your case. I'll see that you get delivery in three weeks. Is that all right, Mr Curtis?'

(c) 'These showcards are very expensive, and we are allowed to leave them only when we receive orders in gross lots, but because I am so sure you will succeed in selling this line, I'll make you a concession: You can have the showcard for a trial order of six dozen.'

(d) 'I'm afraid that we don't usually supply fixing brackets – you can get these from your local ironmonger. But as this is the first time we have done business together, I'll make a concession and arrange for you to have the brackets free...'

Selling proprietary products

Although all the closing techniques apply to every type of business, there are some additional ways of closing an order if you are selling proprietary products.

When Tom Tudor was sales manager of Wm. Wren Ltd, he told me the following:

One of the big dangers in selling proprietary products to retailers is that of getting into a rut in your approach. The men who are able to maintain a fresh and alert attitude do so because they are able to bring the interest to it that springs from complete knowledge of all techniques of salesmanship. Closing the sale is, to them, a fascinating study, which never ends.

They are constantly seeking for ways of improving their technique, and continually refreshing their memory on the fundamentals of successful selling.

For instance, they make a point of being able to use at least five different closes at any one interview, should it prove necessary. An analysis of many hundreds of successful sales has revealed one vital conclusion, which is: the salesman who produces the good figures never gives in too easily. No matter how adamant the buyer may at first appear, they are able to ask for the order in a friendly, natural sort of way, without appearing over-persistent.

The trial close

A 'trial' close is usually in the nature of a question which seems to imply that the salesman takes the order for granted. If the customer does not contradict, or make any adverse comment, it is taken as his tacit consent to the order.

Here are some examples of 'trial closes':

1 'Do you sell more of the large size or the small?'
2 'My experience shows that demand is in the ratio of three black to two brown and one yellow. How does that fit in with your trade, Mr Trelawney?'
3 'Which sizes are you low on?'
4 'Which of your wholesalers will be making deliveries first?'
5 'Ms Fitzgerald, this product is packed, ready for display. I think you'll find that it will pay you to put it on your counter as soon as it arrives.'
6 'Our goods are always very carefully packed, but should any of them arrive damaged, let us know right away and we'll rush an immediate replacement to you.'
7 'Now this is the type of window notice that will show your customers that you are going to stock this line. . .'

These questions and comments help to build the right

sort of atmosphere, making it easy for the salesman to close the order. The men who book high numbers of orders day after day, week after week, year after year, are those who have deliberately drilled themselves into the habit of inserting trial closes at *frequent intervals* into their presentations. They are continually on the alert for signs that the customer is ready to order. Once the customer indicates his willingness, they get down straight away to a discussion of the assortment, thus giving themselves *more time to build up the order*.

Here are some of the techniques they use to build up their orders to a comprehensive range of their products:

1 Running through the price list line by line with the customer.
2 Personal checks of the customers' stocks.
3 Making a point of explaining to the customers how they miss business and disappoint people by being out of stock of any size or colour.

   They point out that the prospect's customers expect him to carry a reasonable variety of choice. If he disappoints them, they will not only go elsewhere to buy that particular item, but, while they are about it, they buy other products as well, so he loses both ways.
4 They make a habit of discussing the proportionate order between two sizes, colours, or varieties, thus ensuring that the stocks are in correct proportion to the demand.
5 They make use of topical influences such as holidays, altered journey schedules, increased demand for seasonal products, new advertising campaigns, etc.
6 They never hesitate to place before their customers *in writing* the extra profits which will accrue to them from better discounts on a larger variety.

7   They are sincere in their endeavours to assist the
    trader to calculate reasonably accurately the sales
    potential of the line in his shop.
8   They sell to sell again. They do not overload the
    retailer, but help him to move the goods faster by
    advising and assisting him with display. The techni-
    que of display work – 'merchandising', as it has
    come to be known in this country – is a separate
    subject. Suffice to say, however, that salesmen who
    are intent on building up the size of their orders in
    the proprietary product business must always give
    due attention to this integral aspect of their duties.
    Failure to do this may mean that the return journey
    will reveal a heavy proportion of the stocks still
    unsold.

My experience has been that all the leading salesmen
in the proprietary products business have one thing in
common when it comes to clinching the sale. They
convey the impression to the trader that their sole
anxiety is to meet *his needs* – and that should be their
aim. Moreover, they so word their conversation that
their customer is made to think of the goods moving *out*
of his shop, not coming *in*.

Get the decision

You can use any combination of these closing techniques. You can summarise and then close on a minor
point; you can offer a concession, and then close on an
alternative. But if you use these techniques in a positive
manner – if you will always ask for the order – you will
undoubtedly close more orders and get more decisions.

Although I have referred throughout this chapter to
closing sales, the same rules apply to obtaining any
decision. Often you will call on a buyer or prospective

buyer with the objective of obtaining a decision to allow you to use his name for advertising purposes, to persuade him to attend an exhibition, to ask him to install a test unit, to get the views of his customers, etc. Whatever the decision, however, if you use any combination of the closing techniques, and if you always *ask for the order*, you will be sure to achieve outstanding results.

10 Closing on the first call

Although the first occasion on which a salesman meets
a buyer is when he should try his hardest to obtain the
order, this of course is not possible when negotiating
for large contracts, or when plans have to be drawn up
or committees confronted. However, when that salesman finally meets the person who can give him a
decision, that is the time when he should fight hardest
to close the sale. When I refer to orders on the first call
therefore, I mean the first occasion when the salesman
is able to explain his full sales story, with the possibility
of obtaining the order.

I remember a brilliant salesman, now an executive,
who, on presenting his plans to a board of directors,
closed the order on the spot for a contract of some
£50,000. At the meeting the managing director, after
some discussion, told the salesman that he would no
doubt be placing the order, and he would write to him
later confirming this, but the salesman then suggested
that it would be just as easy for him to sign his
company's order form there and then, or dictate his
acceptance of the tender immediately, which would
save time and help with delivery.

Later the salesman met a competitor, who told him
that he had called just a day after the order had been
placed. That competitor might well have obtained the
business if the salesman had not been determined to get
the order on that first opportunity to close the sale.

The average salesman, however, is not faced with the difficulties of negotiating contracts. Generally, when he sees his prospect for the first time, he is in a position to close the sale. The only reason for so many buyers asking for a letter to be written is to rid themselves of the salesman.

The other standard excuse, as we know, is 'Put it in writing'. I do want to impress upon you not to be so eager in the future to agree to the 'put it in writing' request.

A story of Egypt

Professor McKetchly tells the story of a tragedy he uncovered during his excavations in Egypt a few years ago. One day he came across a skeleton, fairly well preserved, and by its side were many blocks of stone closely covered with hieroglyphics. The bones had been there for thousands of years.

Because it was so long ago it took him many months to unravel the message. First, he had to decipher the hieroglyphics, then he had to put two and two together; then four and four, until eventually the story was complete.

Apparently the skeleton had once been a man who was a salesman in very ancient Egypt. He had evidently invented a new system for cutting corn, and had tried to sell it to a farmer. He had not obtained an order on the spot, but had been told to put his whole proposition in writing. Back at home he went to work. But typewriters had not yet been thought of in those days and he could only convey his message by cutting out the words on stone tablets. It took him six or seven weeks to hew out his sales letter.

He was half-way through his lengthy proposal when he heard that the farmer had bought a similar contrivance elsewhere. The poor fellow died of a broken heart.

Think about this story, because since then thousands and thousands of salesmen have had their hearts broken by prospects who use the old gag, 'Write me a letter'.

The reason why

I hope this story of ancient Egypt will catch your imagination and will be remembered by you when confronted by a buyer who says, 'Write me a letter'. If your company has provided you with an adequate order form, usually all the buyer needs to have in a letter can be written on that form.

Don't telephone

Sometimes when you are attempting to close an order on that first call, the prospect, apparently all in favour of your offer, concludes, 'Ring me to-morrow and I'll tell you what we want'.

Never, never telephone. It is so easy to say 'No' over the telephone. Whenever a prospect tells you to telephone him, call instead.

11 Objections

This story will stay in your mind and help you to lose all fear of those last-minute objections. So many salesmen have said to me, 'All was going well and then he said, "I'm not happy about..."'

Well, here is the story.

It was told by Polski, the famous lion-tamer. He it was who, when working with five lions, put part of his head into the mouth of one of them, rode another across the circus ring, wrestled with a third, and made all the kings of the jungle do his bidding at the twitch of a whip, or by pointing his renowned gold-topped, black walking stick at them.

When asked by a journalist if he had no fear, he replied, 'None whatsoever, because I always remember the two rules: one is never to turn my back on a lion. So long as I am facing the lions I am not fearful. The second, and more important rule is, always be one step ahead of the animal. Know exactly what he is going to do next. If ever the day comes when a lion is one step ahead of me, that will be the end of my career as a lion-tamer'.

Read that story again and memorise it. Then say to yourself, 'I shall fear no objection if I am always one step ahead of my prospect or customer. If either is ever one step ahead of me, it may not be the end of my career, but it will certainly be the end of that particular sale.

The best technique for overcoming this problem is not to let the objection arise. Nobody minds switching thoughts – most of us do it all the time. As others talk, explain, lecture, we often want to interrupt. Later, however, when our doubts have been removed, we are glad that we remained silent. Once we have spoken out, we try to justify ourselves, right or wrong. When a buyer voices his objection, it becomes doubly hard to persuade him to change his mind, and he will sometimes use ridiculous arguments rather than admit that he is wrong.

The objective of the salesman when devising his sales offer is to forestall objections, so avoiding a subsequent clash of ideas, with each buyer determined to sustain his objection.

When my company first entered the training field, there were already two well-established training organisations. Neither took very kindly to our competing with them. Whether it was they, or others, who spread the rumour about us, I don't know. What I do know is that regularly, when we contacted prospective buyers, we were told, 'Oh yes, you're the Americans who teach high-pressure selling, aren't you? We're not too keen on American selling tactics over here'. Possibly it is because we were so successful that the story was spread around that we were trying to inculcate into British salesmanship ideas foreign to the Anglo-Saxon heritage.

Today of course none of this applies, but long ago sales executives in this country were very much biased against the US selling techniques. We pre-empted this objection by telling a sporting story. At that time one of England's greatest Test cricketers was Patsy Hendren. My brother and I were born in Chiswick, and the local cricket pitch was at Turnham Green. As a teenager I used to play there, and Patsy Hendren would, whenever possible, turn out as a member of the local team.

It was he who told us on one occasion, 'Batting is all about remembering basics; but it is also about knowing in advance the strengths and weaknesses of the opposing team – their bowlers and their batsmen'.

Why did we tell that story whenever possible? To let the buyer know that the Tack brothers were both born in Chiswick, played for a local cricket team, and were therefore in no way connected with the USA. The bias was countered before its influence could take effect. You strengthen your case immeasurably when you consider all possible objections, and then take steps to obviate them, or lessen their impact by including the answers in your sales presentation.

Forestalling the objection

The completed list of objections and answers should be studied in conjunction with the sales offer analysis forms. Consider each feature/benefit, to determine whether or not the YOU appeal sentence should be altered to counter a possible objection.

For example, you are selling a piece of equipment which is noisy, and an objection to the noise is raised at nearly every call. To quieten the unit, however, would entail extra costs, and in the opinion of the marketing director the benefits you can offer far outweigh the noise factor.

In your sales offer you have already stressed the benefits of reduced oil consumption, etc., but the buyer, having perhaps been primed by a competitor, may say, 'That's all very well, but what about our operators who have to stand by the machine all day? The noise will drive them up the wall!'

What you must do is slightly change the YOU appeal benefit sentence before the objection arises. You could say something like this: 'Mr Chandler, the Star equip-

ment, as you probably know, has been specially designed to give you reduced consumption of oil, while, at
the same time, stepping up production; and this is
achieved without excessive noise. We have not silenced
the unit at your expense, as we could so easily have
done. This would only add to the cost for no real
purpose...' You must not, then, pause for comment
from the buyer, but continue to prove the savings, and
later seek a 'Yes' response.

Having put the issue in its true perspective, you have
reduced the mountain of noise to a molehill in the
buyer's mind, and when you re-emphasise the saving in
cost due to the rational thinking of your design, or R &
D department, you take the sting out of a competitor's
claim, while discounting the noise factor. If it were not
for the competitor's claim the buyer would perhaps not
have raised the objection at all.

If you are selling tubing, you could regularly be met
with the objection, 'I can get exactly the same from X;
there is no need for me to open a new account'. Once
more you may be able to forestall the objection during
your presentation by saying, 'Mr Hewlett, I am not
claiming that our tubing is less expensive or more
expensive than any other. But I can claim that with us
you are assured of outstanding service, which has to be
experienced to be appreciated. We...' By emphasising
early in the sales offer the outstanding service your
company gives, you may remind a buyer that the
standards of his present suppliers are not as good as
they may have been in the past.

Many salesmen regularly meet with the objection,
'Sorry, but I want immediate delivery, I can get them
quicker elsewhere'. If you know you can't deliver your
products quickly, it would be wrong to make any rash
promises, but you can include in your presentation, 'I
know, Mr Thomas, that you will want deliveries as
quickly as possible, but I also know that nothing would

get past you if it were not manufactured to the highest standards. Our quality product has to pass through six separate tests. When we deliver in nine weeks' time, you will not need to waste your time carrying out further tests. They are guaranteed by us. . .'

Here is another example. A possible objection may be, 'The typists in the office complain that the new chairs give them backache. I can't order any more until you come up with the answer'.

That salesman could build into his sales presentation the following:

> I want to mention one point which will interest, and please you. As you know, buyers of electric shavers are always told that it may take three or four months before the skin becomes adapted to the change. Something similar applies to office chairs. Our chairs have the approval of leading orthopaedic surgeons, but from their experience they have told us that it will take some little time for those using the chairs for the first time to become used to them. If one or two of your typists have still not got settled into them, explain that in a few weeks' time they will realise the benefits of using our orthopaedically designed chairs. I'll leave you a few of these leaflets, as they will convince any doubters.

That suggestion, built into the presentation, may well arouse discussion, but it will not be controversial, as it would have been if the objection had been raised by the buyer.

A fire-extinguisher salesman knows that it is a large object, and prospects may complain of its size. He says, 'Miss Longstaff, one of the advantages of our extinguishers is their size. Because they are fairly large, and robustly built, they hold 50 per cent more water than the average extinguisher – the extra amount you may need to kill a fire completely. And they can easily be seen – everyone knows where they are. So many smaller types are put away in a drawer, and no one can find one when it is wanted. You like this design, don't you, Miss Longstaff?'

Delaying the decision

The delay objection is not, on the face of it, an objection against buying, but only against arriving at an immediate decision.

Here are some examples:

1 'I want to think about the fixing problem again. Come and see me next week.'
2 'I shall have to see my partner (co-director, mana- ger...) because he has to be consulted about the design of this job (or about buying canned merchan- dise, electrical goods...)
3 'It's over our budget; I shall have to put it before the board.'
4 'Although your offer seems right, there are other factors which still have to be considered...'
5 'As it might mean a change in our production line, I must speak to R & D first.'
6 'As it is partly to do with transport, I must discuss it with Mr Neville.'

In reply to the last example the salesman could say something like this: 'I appreciate that Mr Neville must be consulted, but if at this moment the decision were solely yours, would you place the order?'

If the buyer is hesitant, or gives a negative reply, the salesman will know that he has not proved his case. He will then have to discover the real reason why the buyer will not arrive at an immediate decision. Generally, however, the buyer using a delay objection is avoiding a decision. He is not sure, so he wants to think things over.

But surely the thinking time is when he is with the salesman – when he can ask questions, and clear his mind of doubts. The problem facing the salesman is to discover a buyer's real reason for delaying his decision – which can, so often, be to find out what competitors have to offer.

Here are some answers to delay objections:

(a) 'I appreciate, Mrs Garrett, that you would like to leave matters for two or three weeks, but what is there to think over? Perhaps I haven't explained everything clearly to you. Let me go through again all the reasons why this product can be of service to you, and perhaps you will tell me if there is any point that is not clear to you.'

(b) 'Mr Jackson, I do understand your reason for delaying a decision. Before I started this job I had six months of intensive training, and I have now been with the company for five years. All this has helped me to give a better service to our customers; it also means that I have been trained to explain fully to you every facet of our service.'

(c) 'No doubt you would prefer me to address your board, so as to be sure that they have all the facts. You wouldn't want a negative response, owing to my not being present to answer questions, would you?'

(d) 'Mr Somerville, you are in business to make profits, isn't that right? When this equipment is installed, you will make extra profits right away.'

(e) 'Let us take a small amount of £200 profit in six months. (This may be from extra turnover, reduced absenteeism, or labour costs, etc.) It would

mean that our equipment, which now costs £1,000,
will cost you £1,200 in six months, because we must
then include the £200 that you will have lost.'

(f) 'You are a man of decision, Mr Forsyte. Don't you
think it right for you to decide now?'

(g) 'Miss Chandler, you have built up your business by
making decisions – decisions based on facts. I have
given you the facts, and so I know you, like Mr
Whiting of Stevens & Co., will place your order
right away. As I told you, he is delighted with his
purchase – and so will you be.'

All delay objections, if genuine, are raised early in
the sale. When discussing design, a buyer will explain
why he will have to discuss the offer with the R & D
department, his project engineer, or his chief buyer. A
change in the production line will obviously concern
others – possibly trade union officials. But if these
delay reasons (not objections) are *not* made clear early
in the sale, the buyer usually has no reason to delay
buying.

If he is apparently satisfied on all points of the sales
offer, but still says, 'Leave me a leaflet' (catalogue,
drawing, etc.), then he is most certainly not satisfied
with one or more of the features of the product or service.
There is always a reason for the delay excuse, and the
reason is usually one that the buyer does not want to
disclose to the salesman. It is a *hidden objection*.

Yes, buyers do hide their true objections from
salesmen, time and time again. That is why they
occasionally seem to act irrationally.

What perturbs a salesman is that in spite of a good
presentation and getting 'Yes' responses, a buyer will
say, 'No, leave it for a week or so'. At such a moment
many salesmen do not know what action to take. They
have answered every objection the buyer has raised,
except one: the one the buyer is hiding from them.

It is said of Talleyrand, the French diplomat well versed in the double-talk of politicians, that when he was told that a foreign envoy would not be arriving at a conference because he had died on the way, he answered, 'Yes, but I wonder what was the real reason for his not coming!' Let us consider what a salesman can do to find the real reason for the delay objection.

He can say, 'I appreciate, Mr Oliver, that you would like to leave the matter over for two or three weeks, but what is there to think over? Perhaps I haven't explained everything clearly. . .' The reply he will nearly always receive will be, 'No, you have done very well, everything is clear. Leave it for now. . .'

When a salesman knows early in the sales offer that someone else has to be consulted over the buying decision, he will of course ask to be allowed to see that person (committee, board). But when he is not sure of the validity of the objection, he might again try for a decision. The answer will invariably be, 'You can leave it to me. I have all the facts at my fingertips, and I promise I'll do the best I can for you'.

The buyer won't, because he is not sure himself whether or not he should buy. He has an objection unanswered, because he has hidden it from the salesman.

The effective technique you can use to find the hidden objection is to invite the buyer to finish a sentence – a sentence which instinctively he will assume is based on knowledge. When a buyer is unexpectedly asked to voice a thought in this way, you will hear the truth more often than not.

The technique is based on a key phrase: 'And your *other* reason for not deciding now is. . .?' Look straight at the buyer while you are speaking, and begin the sentence on a low note, finishing with a slightly higher inflection.

This technique must not be used at any time other

than at the close. It would be quite wrong to seek the
hidden objection earlier in the sale, when the buyer has
not heard the complete sales offer. In addition, it is
important that the exact words are used; to change
them to, 'Is there any other reason why you are
delaying buying?' would inevitably bring a negative
reply. The direct question which invites a 'Yes' or 'No'
will usually get a 'No'.

If a salesman is continually meeting a delay objection, it is because:

1   The sales offer is incomplete.
2   The salesman doesn't ask for the order. When the
    time arrives, he is too timid to request a decision,
    leaving it to the buyer to say something – and
    usually the buyer raises a delay objection.
3   The salesman has not built confidence. Then the
    buyer, in his turn, becomes timid, fearful of making
    a mistake, and so delays matters.
4   There is a hidden objection, which the salesman has
    not been able to discover.

The price objection

There is no magic answer to the buyer who says, 'You
are too expensive – I can buy cheaper'. There are of
course selling platitudes which are used regularly by
salesmen, but they rarely work. For example: 'Do you
always buy the cheapest, Mr Grant – the cheapest suit,
the cheapest car...?'; 'Nothing is so expensive as
something that is cheap!'; or 'There is nothing manufactured that someone else can't produce more cheaply'.

Although these often-repeated sentences rarely help,
well-thought-out answers are essential in helping to
overcome a price objection. But, first, a salesman
should study the reasons why buyers react unfavour-

ably to price and, equally important, he must analyse his own thinking on the subject.

The salesman and the price objection

Under normal trading conditions most salesmen face price objections continually – not necessarily because a buyer believes he can buy more cheaply, but because he wants to obtain a discount, if possible. Unfortunately, however, too many salesmen believe that they are singled out, and their products condemned, because of the pricing policies of their companies.

Is there a sales manager anywhere in the world who has not been told by a salesman that he is being priced out of the market? (Our training organisation has associate companies world-wide, and everywhere the price objection is always of the utmost concern to salesmen.) Sometimes a salesman's fear of price is quite irrational, but while positive thinking won't help him much – *my price is not too high, my price is not too high* – negative thinking – *my price is too high, everyone knows my price is too high* – is disastrous.

First, then, every salesman should decide how to defeat his own fear of the price objection. He should begin by asking himself two questions:

1 Would my company still be in existence if our products were so over-priced?
2 As I have been taking orders at our standard prices, why should those buyers be so incompetent as to buy from me if they can buy better elsewhere?

The next step in defeating the price bogey is for a salesman to meet a salesman employed by one of his competitors. This is not difficult, because salesmen meet each other all the time – on trains, in waiting-rooms, in car parks. . .

He should ask the other salesman this question: 'Why do you always undercut prices?'

Back will come the reply, instantly: 'Well, I like that! My company undercut prices? That really is the pot calling the kettle black! It's your people who keep making special offers'.

If only salesmen could attend sales conferences of other companies, in any field of activity, they would find that at question time there will always be someone who will raise, and condemn, the pricing policy.

The successful salesman is quite proud of the fact that he does not compete on price, although he does compete very strongly on value. He will say to a buyer, 'Not only does the Comet give you all these benefits, but in addition we guarantee a twenty-four-hour service. And the price is *only*. . .' because he believes that the price is relatively low, compared with the value he is offering.

Remember, it is always value which determines the price the buyer will pay.

The buyer and the price objection

It is a buyer's function to spend his company's money to the best advantage. His first consideration is to fill the exact need at the lowest possible price.

A salesman can influence the minds of such buyers as follows:

1 By re-stressing the value of the long life of the product.
2 By stressing the quality of the product.
3 By stressing the value of the service.

It is said that a dog can tell instinctively if a human being is afraid. Good buyers certainly have a sense which tells them whether or not they can take advantage of a salesman's fear of price. Buyers have told us over and over again that although they always feel it is a part of their job to raise the price objection, they are also sending out a challenge: *convince me that it is in my interests to pay your price*.

When to introduce the price

It is possible on many occasions to forestall a price objection if a salesman is able to heap benefit on benefit before he gives the price. Although that should be the salesman's aim, whenever he is asked the price by a buyer, he must not stall. Hesitation could be taken as a reluctance to give the price because it is too high.

The only exception to this rule is if the price cannot be given until a survey has been made, additional information obtained, or it is necessary to have a better understanding of a buyer's exact needs. Only then may the salesman answer, 'I can't tell you exactly now, because. . .' or 'The price will depend on. . .' His objective, however, must be to give as many benefits as possible *before* introducing, or being asked for, the price.

Answering the price objection

Whether the price objection is used by a buyer to attempt to obtain an extra concession, or in the genuine belief that he could buy better, handling the objection is the same. The salesman must concentrate the mind of the buyer on price difference.

For example, a salesman quoting ten units at a total price of £1,200 may be told by the buyer that he can buy similar units for £1,000. The salesman says: 'Mr Ambrose, it is true that our price is £120 a unit, and the price you want to pay is £100 a unit; but think what you will be getting for that extra £20 – and it is only £20. a unit. Firstly, we guarantee. . .'

The salesman then goes on to stress the advantages of his products over any similar product the buyer can purchase. Always pinpoint the *difference* in price, and make sure that your benefits outweigh that difference.

What does it cost?

In almost every sales situation the price must be justified. This of course is always true when it is overtly raised. 'It's too expensive' is a typical comment, and it cannot pass unchallenged. Every sales is an investigation, and it is vital to pinpoint the reasons underlying a buyer's opinion. For example, it is always reasonable to query the word 'expensive'. What does it mean? Expense is not an absolute, and makes sense only in relation to another figure.

Here is an example: 'Ms Cummings, you say it is too expensive – and you would appear to be right. I agree with you that it costs more than other products, but when you say expensive, please tell me – in comparison with what?' The buyer's answer gives a basis for discussion. Through product knowledge, an awareness of the customer's needs and of the performance of competitive products, an objective comparison can be made. The process of cost justification can begin. Salesmen should use the word 'cost'; it sounds more professional, and suggests investment rather than spending.

In discussion, and particularly in answer to the question 'How much is it?', a salesman should use 'It costs *only*...' This indicates clearly and simply the salesman's confidence in the offer he is making.

The price objection, like any other, must be answered in terms of benefits. The cost of the product/service, irrespective of the amount, must be shown to be a valuable investment for the purchaser.

Service

A constant factor of any offer is service. The support of the distributor is a specialised form of service, but it exists in many other forms.

The advice of a technical representative is *service*.

The activity of the manufacturers' design staff on behalf of a potential customer is *service*.

The training of customers' staff in the correct operation of newly installed equipment is *service*.

Each element of value must be fully explained, and the buyer must understand how it will benefit him. Not only must he understand, but he must accept that the additional cost is justified in terms of value.

Pride of price

There are two types of salesmen – those who are scared of quality and those who are scared of price. If a salesman is selling a cheap, shoddy article, he is conscious of this and he sells badly.

Now I sympathise with that salesman, because if a man is only selling on price, he can have a tough time indeed. But a salesman selling a good commodity should never be afraid, however high the price may be.

One way of overcoming this nervousness is for the salesman to be proud of the price he charges. When the price query was raised at a meeting of salesmen selling office equipment, the leading salesman said, 'I bring the price up myself in this way: "You know, sir, we're dearer than every competitor – but look at the value we are offering you!"'

That man is proud of his price. You should be the same.

The loyalty objection

This objection will be met by nearly all salesmen selling repeatable products (component parts, chemicals, oils, packaging materials, accessories, consumer goods, consumer durables, etc.). It is usually only encountered at a first call and is possibly the most difficult of all objections to overcome.

Here are some buyers' reasons for their reluctance to change suppliers:

1   'We've been with Ferguson & Co. for thirty years – I've been dealing with them myself for fifteen years, and before that our managing director who, in those days, did his own buying, formed a friendly relationship with Tom Ferguson. They have always given us good service, so there is no point in my changing suppliers at the moment. Of course, if ever things were to alter. . .'

2   'We are one of Brown and Company's largest customers and, no doubt because of this, they look after us very well. We have only to telephone and they will do everything they can to give us express delivery, or accept the return of unsuitable goods. If ever they should let me down I might be prepared to consider. . .'

3   'It's a case of we buy from them, they buy from us. That's fair enough, isn't it? I see no point in changing. . .'

These objections stem not so much from loyalty, although this does play a part, but from confidence in a supplier who has given good service over a number of years.

Why should a buyer change when, over a period of time, he has had no real cause for complaint? A buyer will only make an immediate change if another supplier can offer similar value plus extra benefits – better price, better delivery, better design, or something new. With repeatable products a sudden great advantage of one supplier over another is rare, but no salesman can admit defeat when meeting this very difficult objection, and there are practical actions that he can take. First, he must remember the selling axiom: *when all things are equal, the buyer buys from the salesman he likes best*.

This should remind him to check up on himself – not because his aim is to ingratiate himself with the buyer, but to make sure that he does not annoy the buyer in any way. That could be a mistake made by the opposition, especially if their salesman on the territory is changed.

In any event, over a number of years the regular suppliers are apt to take a buyer for granted, while if they employ a newcomer to the territory, he may not know, or may forget, that his objective at each call is to sell. He may become lackadaisical, or offhand, and antagonise not only the buyer but also other members of the staff.

A salesman's efforts to please a buyer may not result in an order on the first call, or even possibly on the third, fifth, or sixth call. But eventually the buyer's mind can be influenced by the salesman's friendly personality, by his enthusiasm, and because he is so obviously keen to obtain the business.

Now here are some more positive steps the salesman can take:

1 He must have an objective at each visit and never make the call hoping that something will turn up – the '*anything for me to-day*' type of approach.
2 Even at the risk of becoming boring, at each call he should say to the buyer something like this:

    (a) 'I really do appreciate the reason for your loyalty to Douglas & Co., but as I have told you before, it is my ambition for us to have the same opportunity as Douglas's had so many years ago – the opportunity to prove to you that we can offer a similar, although naturally I feel that it will be a better, service. . .'

(b) 'Mrs Harvey, it is impossible to read the future, but imagine a tragedy happening – perhaps a part of Jordan's factory burning down. Fires happen all the time; or there could be a strike. . . Wouldn't you like to know that in such an event you had another trusted supplier to help you over a difficult period? Naturally when things were right again you would want to return to Jordan's, and that, I think, would be only fair. We are only aiming for a part of your business. If you will test us now under normal conditions, you will be able to prove for yourself that. . .'

To obtain a share of worthwhile business from a buyer who refuses to open a new account, a salesman must have patience and perseverence, sell benefits on each call, and sooner or later he will get the business. Why? Because the majority of salesmen calling on that supplier will give up too readily, or make a series of 'anything for me to-day?' calls.

The turnround

Few salesmen have not experienced the retort from a prospect or buyer, 'You are the fourth man I've seen to-day with. . .' The right answer to this is, 'Yes, sir, that's only natural. In such an up to date shop (office, factory. . .) as yours, obviously any salesman selling this equipment would know that at some time or another you are going to install (buy, stock) scales. That is why salesmen will keep calling you. I am here now with the best offer...'

Turn the prospect's objection into your own advantage. The about-turn answer

With this method you turn the objection into a sales point, by using the phrase, '*But that is the very reason why you should buy*'.

1   'You don't think that your shop is in the right position for this equipment, madam, but that is the very reason why you should buy, because only by attracting more attention to your shop will you be able to turn this into a busy corner, and make people come to you.'
2   'It's true that delivery cannot be effected for twelve months, and you could, as you say, put the matter off because there can be no hurry, but that is the very reason why you should place your order now, sir. Things will not become any easier, they will get worse. What will your feelings be if you want to buy next year, and delivery is then two years ahead?'
3   'I appreciate, sir, that your district might not be right for this type of product, but that is the reason why you should buy it, because by doing so you will be creating a new market. You will turn those people who have never thought of buying it before into buyers. If you don't give them a chance to buy, then you will never be able to create additional sales.'

Techniques for handling objections

1   *Don't interrupt*. All too often salesmen do not allow the buyer to complete his objection. Because a

salesman is so sure that he knows what the buyer is
thinking and believes he has the answer, he interrupts and, by doing so, never hears the complete
objection. For example, the buyer may say, 'Yes,
that's all very well, but the lining. . .' The salesman,
feeling sure that the buyer is concerned about the
strength of the manmade fibres used in the lining,
interrupts with, 'Please don't worry about the lining, Mrs Oliver, we can strengthen it by using an
interlining as well'. The salesman may thus have put
into the mind of the buyer a query about the quality
of the lining, when perhaps, the buyer only wanted
to criticise the texture, colour, finish. . .

The buyer should always be allowed to give his
objection in full. He or she must not be interrupted,
and, equally important, the salesman must look as
though he is deeply interested in the buyer's comments.

When you listen carefully to the buyer's complete
objection he or she will give more attention to your
answer.

2   When an objection has been answered, don't refer
to it again.

3   For a salesman to be certain that he fully understands an objection, it is sometimes wise to repeat
it.

4   *The apparent agreement technique.* We know that a
relaxed buyer decides more readily. We know that
tensions build up in a buyer just before he comes to
a decision, and often before making an objection.
He makes his point, and waits for the skirmish to
begin. But no salesman wants a battle and if he is
unable to forestall the objection, he must try to
remove the tension from the buyer. By using the
apparent agreement technique he indicates that he is
inclined to agree with the objection and the buyer,
thinking he has won his point, relaxes.

Remember that the salesman only *apparently* agrees. If the buyer raises an objection that the price is too high and the salesman answers, 'Yes, it is high but. . .', the buyer may relax, but the salesman will find it very hard to convince him that the price is right, having once agreed with the buyer. The emphasis on *apparently* agreeing, e.g. 'I can understand, Mr Quincy, your thinking at this stage that the extra investment may not be worthwhile, but. . .'; 'On the face of it, Mr Latimer, it does seem right that extra labour might be needed, but. . .'; 'Your concern about the viscosity of the oil, Mr Maguire, is understandable, but. . .'; or 'I quite see your point of view, Miss Gaskell, and I'm glad you raised it, but. . .'

Remember, the apparent agreement technique relaxes the buyer, slows down the pace of the sale, does not make a salesman appear too clever. Furthermore, it shows courtesy, because the salesman apparently appreciates the buyer's point of view.

The all-important techniques

A salesman may know the answer to every objection that could be raised, but if he pounces, appears glib, argues, and doesn't use the *apparent agreement* technique, his knowledge will be of little use to him. *Never*, however experienced you are, use such a statement as, 'I've been in this business for thirty years and I can tell you that. . .' No buyer likes to be made to look foolish or ignorant.

To succeed in selling, the techniques for answering objections are almost as important as the possession of a storehouse of answers to every objection.

12 Sometimes we are all difficult

Most buyers are reasonable people who can be influenced by a good sales presentation. The main difference between the good and the average salesman is that the first-class salesman gets orders from customers with whom the average salesman makes little headway.

What we must all understand is that whenever we are buyers, or professional buyers are at decision time, we can both be difficult because of the fear of making a mistake, and to frustrate a salesman we both develop acts. When you meet difficult buyers, you must prepare yourself for their acts so that you can counter them.

The talkative buyer

This buyer's defence mechanism is his ability to talk nonstop. The sales presentation becomes bogged down, and if the buyer has his way, never emerges.

The talkative buyer will sidetrack the salesman, by giving his opinion of the headlines in the daily papers, sport, politics, the difficulties he encounters with management. . . Then he will move over to his hobbies. He will also reminisce – 'Do you remember. . .', he begins, but never waits for a response from you. He remembers all right! After a while this buyer will conclude, 'I'm rather busy this morning. Can you leave that brochure (sample – photograph – drawing. . .) and I'll be in touch. . .?'

To overcome this spate of words the salesman must interrupt. I appreciate that this advice is contrary to that given earlier, when the salesman was told that he must not pounce, but must always let the buyer finish his story. But there are exceptions to every rule, and the talkative buyer is one of those exceptions. He must be interrupted without obvious discourtesy.

'That's a most interesting point you have made, Mr Stanley. I hear the same story so often about accountants dictating to buyers. This usually follows so much form filling – that's why I believe I can help you. . .'; or, 'Mr Lyle, forgive me for interrupting you, but you have just made a most important point; important because. . .' Then you go on with the sales story.

The technique will work almost every time, provided the salesman is not weak with his interruption. He must speak strongly, and, without waiting for any response, immediately continue with his sales offer. Once the talkative buyer listens, it is up to the salesman to arouse and maintain his interest. If he does so, the talkative buyer will not talk quite so much. There will then be two-way communication, with every opportunity for an order to result.

The too-friendly buyer

A buyer may be abrupt, ill-mannered, discourteous at times, but he may also listen carefully to a salesman's proposition. That is why the brusque buyer is not too difficult to sell to.

But the too-friendly buyer can make life very hard for the salesman. He has long realised that it is difficult for a salesman to sell when he – the buyer – is being so friendly.

The weak salesman is always impressed with this friendliness. Often he will tell his sales manager how well he has been received, and how he is absolutely certain of an order coming later. But it won't. On the next visit the buyer will be just as friendly. He may say, 'You may rely on me to do all I can for you, but I'm not quite ready yet'.

Only the strength of a salesman's words can win over the too-friendly buyer. When, during the presentation, the strong salesman gets a 'yes' response, he must ask for the order. Maybe he won't get it on that occasion, but he will try again with the next 'yes' response.

The friendlier the buyer becomes, the stronger the salesman sells – again, by using positive words, never negative words. The strong salesman knows that a friendly arm around the shoulders and a 'Thank you for calling' was not the objective of his visit. The only thanks he wants is a signed order. It is always good to have a firm friendship with buyers so that they will want to buy from you, but that is entirely different from the buyer who uses friendship as an act.

The timid buyer

All buyers are scared at some time of making a wrong decision. On such occasions confidence-building must have a high priority in the sales offer. But the timid buyer won't buy unless he has complete confidence in the supplying company. He's always scared of making a mistake.

The timid buyer doesn't want approval of his decision from a higher placed executive, he only wants agreement that he is acting correctly, so that if a mistake is made, he can then say the decision was not just his. Once a salesman has built up trust in himself and his company by the little extra services he gives, he knows that he can rely on the timid buyer being very loyal to him.

Keep on using confidence-building sentences when selling to a timid buyer.

The taciturn buyer

This man says very little. He would rather grunt than say 'Yes', because the grunt is so noncommittal. He is a good listener, except that his listening doesn't seem to bring him any nearer to arriving at a decision.

The technique when selling to him is very similar to that of selling to the compulsive talker. The salesman must keep asking questions. Adroit questioning will force this silent buyer eventually to take an interest in the sale, always provided that the questions are directly pertinent to the buyer's business.

The bluffer

The bluffer says, 'I don't sample – it's either all or nothing for me. What's the use of playing around? We'll put one in every car throughout the fleet, or we won't do anything. I'm all for it, but as you will appreciate, for a decision like this we have to get Board approval. Come back in about two months. There will be a Board meeting before then, and I'll be ready to talk to you'. The salesman happily goes on his way, telling everyone he meets in his family or at the office that he is going to get the biggest order ever in a few months' time.

To win these buyers, never attempt to cut them down to size. Let them cut themselves down.

The salesman can say something like this: 'Mrs Howard, I can see your point of view exactly, and, of course, there is the extra discount when you buy for the whole fleet of cars. But I'd like to make a suggestion which would satisfy me, and may satisfy you: start off with six cars. The drivers will have to be trained in how to use them, and it's easier to train six than 200. And that would only mean an initial outlay of. . .'

The bluff has been called without the bluffer realising it. To strengthen your case, always tell the bluffer of some of the larger organisations which began by trying out in a small way and then built up from there. That will make the bluffer happy – he or she is still the big one, in line with other big ones, making similar decisions.

This advice seems to go against all selling principles – you will read elsewhere in this book how wrong it is to undersell, how wrong it is to take a smaller order when a little more persuasion would bring a large one, and this rule applies to 90 per cent of your calls or more. It only changes when you are facing the bluffer.

But how do you recognise the bluffer? He may have played the game with you before, or he may give himself away by his eagerness to impress you with his determination to buy big, or not at all. Very few normal buyers speak in that manner. Most prefer to buy small, and have to be convinced to buy big. But if ever you have the slightest doubt as to whether you are dealing with a bluffer or not, continue with your presentation and try for the big order. If he has bluffed you once, he won't bluff you a second time.

In the majority of cases you will never get that large order from the bluffer. If he is totally convinced of the need to cover the whole fleet of cars, for example, then he won't attempt to bluff. It is only that he is rarely determined to take such a step.

The busy buyer

The busy buyer is usually not overworked, but whenever

anyone enters his office, it is always a scene of great activity. He does this to impress everyone – his own staff and salesmen – as to how busy he is, which makes him such an important person. He can quickly put off even the best salesman with, 'It's all go, go, go today!'

Remember the axiom: *never attempt to sell under adverse conditions*. Many a salesman, when up against the 'busy' buyer will suggest that he calls again at a more convenient time, but that salesman would be overlooking the corollary to the axiom – *be sure the conditions are adverse, be sure that you are not being led into a trap*.

It is always best to test the 'activity' atmosphere to make sure that the buyer is not putting over an act. To do this the salesman must launch very quickly into a major benefit. In addition, the salesman must make sure to let the buyer know that he is aware of how busy that buyer is. This will give the buyer the opportunity to explain how he is always so busy, how he always has to do everything himself, etc. And while talking in this manner the buyer, is discussing one of his favourite subjects – himself, and the difficulties under which he works, how he has to do the work of three people...

Once having established his importance, this buyer is often prepared to sit back and listen.

The shy buyer

There is a great deal of shyness in the world, and it is strange that someone who buys regularly can still be shy. Such a buyer will not look you in the eyes and will always seem to be interested in everything else in the department other than your sales presentation.

Try and capture this buyer's attention quickly, not only by asking questions but by using a pen and notepad. Try to develop a visual sales presentation, by writing down some figures – calculations, delivery dates – and get the buyer to work with you. If a calculation is required, then get the shy buyer's co-operation. This will help to overcome his shyness.

The sarcastic buyer

The sarcastic buyer is at the top of his form when he has an audience – maybe an assistant in the shop, perhaps a member of his work force, a colleague. He delights in playing to an audience.

You may be tempted to lose your temper with such a person – don't! He is showing off, and using sarcasm as a defence. He may not be such a bad fellow underneath, and if you persist, without showing your anger at his witty comments – he thinks them witty, you think them sarcastic – you will win. He will not stop being sarcastic, but his remarks will lose their sting when he becomes a buyer and not just a sarcastic person.

The old buyer

He has probably been in the business for many years, either on his own account, or working for others. He may not take kindly to new ideas, and he doesn't think very much of modern salesmanship. He lives in the past when he could, with more leisure, select the goods he required.

Often he is a kindly man, and although he may seem irritable on occasion, put this down to his having heard everything before – or perhaps his health isn't as good as it used to be. He always believes the salesman is trying to put something over on him, and talking down to him will lose you any chance of an order.

Do not be clever with this man. Never produce the quick answer. You must respect him for what he is, and for what he has done. You may not see eye to eye with him, but he has vast experience in his line of business. Learn from that experience.

Ask his advice. Show him that you are ready to learn from him much more than he can learn from you. Impress him with your integrity and honesty. Never try to rush him, or force an issue. Prove each point step by step. Never judge him by appearances – he is not like Mr Sarcastic; he may look gruff and frightening, but he could develop into a great friend.

The young buyer

This is a most difficult buyer – the youngster who has risen too quickly. He hates you to think him young and inexperienced; he is scared of making a mistake which would prompt a relative or his chief to wonder if it was right to give such a young man an important position. One day he will learn his business and carry out his job efficiently. Now it is your duty to help him by giving him a complete sales presentation, thus teaching him about your products, so that he can learn more about the goods he is buying.

If you are older, take care to show him the greatest courtesy, and never imply that your experience is superior to his. At the same time, let him teach you something so that you may thank him for his help. You must make him feel less young and inexperienced – this way you will sell to him, and make a good friend of him.

Know your buyers

When you recognise the various types of buyer you will have made your first step towards motivating them to listen, and to be interested in you and your presentation.

13 Negotiating

Negotiating begins when the sales presentation reaches the closing stage, and the buyer begins to look for concessions.

To negotiate a concession, offered or requested, before the buyer is convinced that he needs the product or service being offered can be a waste of time. A buyer may give 'yes' responses throughout the presentation, but then finally demand a change – packs in half-dozens instead of dozens for a shopkeeper, sharp edges rounded off or some other change from standard for an engineer, or a different range of colours for a builder. In addition, there are always demands for price concessions – special discounts, longer credit terms. . . But if a buyer is not convinced in the first place that a product is right for him, then negotiation on such points does not arise.

Do not mislead yourself into believing that the grant of an earlier concession will bring about an early close. Rarely does this happen, so sell first. Give nothing away. Convince the buyer that yours is the answer to his needs, and with that stage complete and the buyer interested, negotiations can begin.

The salesman, if unable to grant a concession fully, may negotiate by asking a concession from the buyer, in return for his giving way. For example:

1   'It's very difficult to change the packaging now, the computerised flowline is set up to pack in dozens. . .

however, if you can double your order, maybe I can persuade our production director to change the system.'
2 'I do see your point about the edges, but the only way we could round them off would be if you could accept a five millimetre decrease in the overall size.'

The buyer may demand sole rights for the area, or that a product be made larger, or smaller; or he will only consider buying if your credit terms can be changed. Some such requests may be valid; others may be a part of the buyer's ploy to send the salesman away to pressurise his management to change this or that, or even to obtain a concession which he did not expect to get – a try-on.

Many a buyer uses this ploy to demand almost impossible concessions, to test out the salesman. The salesman must remember when this happens that he has not lost the order at the negotiating stage, he lost it during his presentation, which was not good enough. However, if a presentation has been of high quality, then the salesman must know how to deal with impossible demands, which can be done by skilful negotiating.

Let us look at the prime negotiating skills, and the knowledge required when the buyer in his turn says, 'Yes, but. . .' Negotiating can be divided into four stages – pre-planning, opening the negotiations, negotiating, and closing.

Pre-planning

Chapter 12 listed examples of difficult buyers. Negotiating brings to light another type of difficult buyer. He is the person who must win a concession to satisfy his ego, and who rarely places an order, unless it is essential to immediate requirements, without making some demands.

To him, winning is everything – just as important as the price he wants reduced or the technical changes he requests. Some companies have a pricing policy which allows for such discount requests – a policy which is most unfair to those buyers who accept the standard pricing structure. It is not considered unethical to build in such an additional discount; in fact, if you are selling to buyers in the Middle East, who always demand such special favours, there seems to be no alternative but to have a built-in allowance for such demands. They won't buy unless they can enjoy the pleasure of having won for themselves a special concession. However, by careful planning, and knowing in advance the type of buyer you are going to meet, you can, by your honest presentation, persuade the buyer to order without giving that extra discount. That is your negotiating aim.

When a presentation contains every conceivable benefit and is expressed with honest enthusiasm, even the most hard-hearted ego-ridden buyer can be won over.

Here are some research strategies:

1 Research into the buyer's background, relations with his staff, technical skills, hobbies, and particularly, his negotiating strategies.
2 Know the parameters of your offer and never go beyond them.

   Never be persuaded by a buyer to telephone your sales manager to request the right to break the rules laid down by the company. This action will only persuade the buyer that he can squeeze something extra from you, otherwise you would never have volunteered to telephone. Moreover, it places your sales manager in a difficult position. If he allows you to go beyond the parameters set, then these limits were wrong in the first place and you were being let down by your sales manager. To telephone is to weaken your case. When you feel the need to do so, whatever the reason, then your pre-planning has been inadequate. (This does not apply to information-seeking calls.)

3   Define your objectives, which may relate to your ideal settlement or to the maximum settlement you will agree.

4   Be realistic. Do not seek the almost impossible, by trying to prove to others how tough you are as a negotiator.

5   If you are almost sure that the buyer will demand your product to be boxed in sixes instead of dozens, then pre-empt the request by explaining the value of boxing in dozens, or get clearance before calling. Even then, remember to make the buyer fight for the concession. His winning will enable you to press for a concession on your side during the negotiations.

6   If you are negotiating with a retailer, you must know in advance what concessions your competitors are offering in the way of special advertising promotions, etc., and must plan to offset these or match them.

7   Always have all the data necessary to support your case.

8   Find out all you can about others who may be brought into the negotiations – assistants, draughtsmen, technicians, secretaries. . . When asked their opinion by a buyer, they can by their answer frustrate all your negotiating objectives. You have to plan how to win them over, paying close attention to their views, if they are present during the negotiating stage, instead of concentrating solely on the buyer. If you ignore them and their views, you may well lose.

9   Write down all the questions and demands you would make if the positions were reversed and you were the buyer.

10 Know exactly the cost of any concession you are allowed to make – then you may not make it so easily!

11 Prepare to define the real issues quickly. Buyers often introduce subsidiary issues to camouflage their main demands.

12 Know the financial situation of the buyer's company as well as that of your own company. What is the cost of your company borrowing money, if it has to give extended credit? If you increase the size of the order, can the buyer's company afford the extra capital?

13 Try to discover quite early in the sale details of other quotations the buyer may have received. This sounds very difficult, and if price is in question, the buyer may try to bluff you into believing he has received a much lower quotation than yours.

Plan the words you will use to persuade the buyer that all you are seeking, in looking at the other quotations, is to point out to him the differences – why your product is more expensive than your competitors and how the benefits of those differences can outweigh the price factor. You can point out that you are both quoting for the same job, but in different ways.

14 What will your answer be to the statement which so often arises, 'You'll have to do better than that'? What is meant by better? Bring the demand down to detail, so that you can show that the difference is only marginal.

Pre-negotiation preparation

Time spent on planning research is never wasted. From this information the basic negotiation can begin.

(a) The *initial stance* is the maximum price you could hope for, but if it is to be credible, it will have to be properly justified.
(b) The *rock bottom* limit is the price level at which you would only just deal. Strictly speaking, it is the level at which you make a sufficient surplus to make some contribution towards your overheads.
(c) The *target price* is the price at which your company gets a sufficient contribution to pay off its over-heads (fixed costs) and still leave an acceptable profit. Within reason, the higher you set the target, the more likely you are to achieve good results.

Having set the limits, now consider what 'variables' can be offered to the buyer. Examples are:

1 Price discounts
    – cash
    – trade
    – quantity.
2 Changes in specification.
3 Credit terms.
4 Currencies.
5 Delivery schedules.
6 Packaging.
7 Other business.
8 Who does what.
9 Extras.

These should be evaluated, firstly, to establish the potential cost and its effect on your target price and, secondly, to estimate the value to your customers. The best concessions are those which cost least and offer most. Search them out in advance.

Opening the negotiations

As we know, negotiations begin when the buyer says,

'Yes, but. . .' The *'but'* means that a concession request is on the way.

Your tactics should be:

1   Listen intently, otherwise you may be missing a sentence and jump to the wrong conclusions. Never interrupt the buyer unless he is a compulsive talker, when you will have to use the techniques set out earlier. Let him raise every point, so that you will be able to adapt your tactics to the true arguments, statements, or requests he has made.

2   Ask questions, so that you are certain you know his demands exactly – otherwise you may give in too quickly, only to discover that the request he has made is only the tip of the iceberg only the beginning of his demands for additional concessions.

    At the opening stage quickly assess the strengths and weaknesses of the buyer's demands – and play on those weaknesses.

3   His opening gambit may be intended to bluff you. If so, call his bluff immediately. He will begin with a minor bluff, which may become a major bluff later. A typical example might be, 'I can get delivery by return from XYZ. Can you match that?' Match it, and you will find that you'll be up against a far greater concession demand later.

4   Make no early concession whatsoever. Appear to be strong in your determination to resist such requests, and make only noncommital responses.

Negotiating

1   What are the motives behind the words he uses? For example, if he says, 'That's my limit', does he emphasise the word 'my'? If so, it might mean that if he refers the matter to his boss, his boss might be persuaded to go beyond that limit.

Again, look for the emphasis when he says, 'I can get a discount of 5 to 7 per cent'. 'Can' is the key word. If he always got such a discount, he would use the word 'always'. He is therefore on weak ground.

'It's a factor worth considering' means that he is moving your way in the negotiations.

When he says, 'I'm concerned at what will happen if you can't meet our delivery dates; there should be a penalty clause', 'concern' and 'should' are the two words you should listen out for. This means that he is not adamant, otherwise he would say clearly, 'There *must* be a penalty clause'.

Another typical remark is, 'My engineers will object'. This means that he doesn't object, and you could negotiate your way out of this one by convincing him that the engineers will benefit from the standard, rather than any change; therefore there is little need for him to refer the matter to them. Moreover, this kind of remark might mean that you will have to return to your sales presentation, as the buyer is using an excuse to end the negotiating at this stage.

When he says, 'I wish I could. . .', that means, 'I can, but I need convincing.'

'Let's talk about it' means 'You give way and I'll buy'.

Another excuse used by buyers during negotiating is, 'It's one of our rules which I can't break'. What he means is 'You conform to our rule and I'll buy'. If this is impossible for you, then you will have to persuade him that you are sure he knows the position and can bend the rules if it is of benefit to his company.

2   Never make a buyer feel foolish because you have highlighted the weaknesses of his case. Always make it appear that he has put forward a very good argument, but. . .

3   When the going gets tough and he appears obdu-
    rate, use the *why* technique. Continually seek
    clarification by asking, 'Why?' Seek justification
    for his requests, again by asking, 'Why?' The *Why*
    technique is a winner.

4   While, during the selling, good humour and friend-
    liness prevail, all is well. But when the negotiating
    begins, tempers can become frayed. Selling is
    clear-cut, with the presentation laying out all the
    benefits, while, to some, negotiation is a game
    which has to be won.
        Because the buyer wants to win so badly he may
    lose his temper when the salesman scores points,
    and will not give way. Salesmen must never retali-
    ate. Let the buyer shout or show his anger in any
    other way. The salesman must remain calm, and
    never lose his temper – not even when the buyer is
    obviously acting unfairly. Answer quietly and con-
    vincingly, but use the 'I agree but. . .' technique
    and you may win. Become angry and you will
    undoubtedly lose.

5   Be completely honest. Never hint that you can pull
    strings, bend rules, be a wheeler-dealer. In the
    long run the buyer will have faith and confidence in
    someone he trusts.

6   If you make a mistake, don't correct yourself
    immediately. If the buyer is able to point out this
    mistake to you, it will make him feel better and
    more important.

7   If you have received permission to make a special
    concession, always hold it back until the close.
    Then you may not need to give it at all.
        In our Consultancy Division we are, at the
    present time, allowed to give certain clients a 50 or
    60 per cent discount, which is paid by the govern-
    ment to help smaller companies. Our salesmen are
    taught never to offer this concession. First, they

win over the client so that he agrees 99 per cent with the offer but may be a little concerned at the cash outlay. Only then do our salesmen mention the government concession.

8 Let the buyer win minor concessions – but never easily. He must always feel that he has won a major victory.

9 Don't be frightened off by a buyer's exaggerated claims. These can apply to deliveries, colour ranges, competitors' offers... Discount such claims by 10 to 50 per cent. Yes, as much as that!

10 Whenever a buyer makes rather wild statements in order to win his point, use the sentence, 'How do you arrive at that figure?'

11 Minimise the concession that the buyer offers on a quid pro quo basis. He must not be allowed to believe that he is offering a major concession.

12 Back to salesmanship! Continue to stress benefits during the negotiating stage – the benefit of making a quick decision because prices might rise, or delivery slow down owing to demand...

13 Reread Chapter 12 on *difficult buyers*. The too-friendly buyer can also be a too-friendly negotiator.

14 Always aim high to begin with. Don't try for a quick victory by lowering the standards set during the preparatory stage.

15 Justify when you cannot give a concession. Never skirt the issue.

16 Keep summarising, to test the buyer's views. Read again Chapter 9 covering 'yes' responses. The same technique applies to negotiating.

Closing

All of the techniques given in Chapter 9 on closing the sale will apply to closing at the negotiating stage.

Here are some additions:

1   Offer that special concession you have been hold-
    ing back. 'I'll concede A, if you'll agree to B...'
2   Offer to split the difference. 'O.K., Miss Baker, we
    can't give you 10 per cent, and you won't agree to 5.
    Make it 7½ per cent and it's a deal!' Be careful,
    however. that that is within the parameters you are
    allowed.
3   Enumerate all the concessions you have already
    made.
4   Don't bluff at the closing stage. If you are going to
    make a final offer, then it must be final – but that is
    a last resort. You only use the word 'final' when you
    are convinced that he is only trying to bluff you.

Your aim

Some negotiating theorists argue that the aim of a
negotiation is a settlement in which both sides retire
gracefully and happily.

Nonsense! You, as a salesman, want to win. You are
employed by your company to win – to give away as
little as possible. Your aim is to increase the profitability of your company, even if that means a little less for
the buyer's company. His aim is the reverse.

Leave him happy by all means. But not because he
has won a big concession – only because he *believes* he
has won, owing to the way you have carried out and
concluded the negotiations.

Your objective is clear. It is not fifty-fifty, it is
sixty-forty – in your favour. If you give way on all his
demands, it will be sixty-forty in the buyer's favour,
and your company may be heading for reduced profits –
even losses.

Only the weak believe they have won a victory when

they have given way to almost every demand made by the buyer. They telephone their offices to change this, change that, demanding special rights on behalf of the buyer. . . The strong salesman aims to give little, win a lot, but still leave the buyer glorying in his apparent victory.

14 Planning and research

In theory, planning and research should have been covered earlier in this book, leading up to selling skills and negotiating. In practice, a salesman can be inspired and enthused to improve his mental attitude, to update his sales presentation, and to master closing techniques, but he can rarely be inspired to plan and research.

Why? Because planning is a chore, and most of us don't like chores. First of all you have to want to succeed in all the selling disciplines; then is the time to discuss the intensive work necessary to plan and research.

The basis of your planning is of course your filing system. If good, it will result in your being able to avoid the stress caused by uncertainty – the stress caused by not being able to remember what happened at a previous visit; the stress of discovering at the interview that you are selling to the wrong person; the stress of criticism from head office, because results are below par; even the stress of forgetting the objective of a call, because each objective must be stated on the card. The objective can be to obtain an order, to obtain a decision to specify, a decision to recommend, a decision to agree delivery arrangements, a decision to agree a joint advertising campaign – or simply a decision to obtain information, such as new buying procedures, new assistants' names, performance of products...

The more you know about a customer before you call, the more likely you are to have a successful interview. You will in fact be mentally attuned to the interview.

Besides your filing cards, you should also have a separate box containing your prospect file. The information listed will be similar to that on the customer file, but will also contain research regarding the prospect's buying habits, competitors' offers, etc.

Trust can be earned by a salesman not making different statements from those made on a previous visit. Promises should always be noted on the card – a broken promise will result in mistrust. It is not good enough for you just to like the customer – he must like you, for your reliability. A poor memory can result in any of us inadvertently letting a customer down. A memory aid stops this happening.

Check before every call, so that you can say with authority, 'You will remember, Mr Hopewell, when I called two months ago you said. . .'; 'Ms Blane, I shan't forget the advice you gave me previously; it has certainly been most helpful. . .'; or 'Mr Murphy, you mentioned on my last visit that you were well stocked, but that you would be ready to buy in about a month's time. It is exactly a month since I called on you. . .'

Our cards

We still have some customer and prospect cards from our early days when we were selling air-conditioning units and Tack Training. In the latter case we not only segmented clients into standard A, B, and C ratings, but also listed those who were in booming industries or who could be in booming industries within the next year or so. This information was gleaned from reading financial magazines, trade magazines, City columns. . .

All the relevant details concerning the booming, or possible booming companies, were written on those prospect or customer cards.

For example, three cards, filled on both sides, dealt with a customer in the car-accessory field and, strange to say, in strong competition with the car manufacturers themselves. The cards listed all details of the managing director, his family, hobbies, an extract from a speech he made to the Institute of Sales Management... Attached to the cards is a newspaper clipping of a letter written by the company's sales manager to a local paper, and there is a resumé of the managing director's views on some of the car manufacturers, plus of course all details of previous bookings at our courses. This mine of information helped us to retain the goodwill of that client for ever after.

Card indexing takes up time – time when you should be helping with the children, gardening, taking your wife out... But good time management – and you will read about this on p. 225, when Eric Pillinger gives his views – can help to find the time for the task.

Otherwise you have to make time sacrifices for your ultimate success.

When you are form-filling, do it with a smile, not with a grumble – not with that pained expression which denotes *what a waste of time*! Do it because it is going to help you, and your future.

Often today people ask me how I find the time to write books, to research books, when I am in control, together with my brother George, of a pretty large business enterprise. The answer is simple: I write for an hour every morning from 6 to 7 o'clock. I write for half an hour after lunch, because lunch takes twenty minutes. And I write in the evening, before I go to bed. It's as simple as that!

It doesn't really hurt, after a while.

Planning for success

The four whats

I read this in a humorous magazine:

> A boxer who has taken a bad beating for several rounds is in his corner waiting for the next round to begin. Before the bell rings, his chief second says to him, 'Right, I've got it! Now this is your plan...'
> The boxer answers wearily, 'This is no time to be making plans'.

That remark could apply just as well to selling. You can't make plans when you are in the shop, office, or factory, battling away for an order. Plans have to be made in advance, and when making them, it is a good idea to remember the four whats. Answer them correctly, and there won't be much wrong with *your* plan of campaign.

1 What is the reason for your making the call?
2 What will the prospect gain by granting you an interview?
3 What can you do to help him?
4 What would be the reason for his buying your product?

Check up regularly on these four whats.

Five questions

Here is a series of questions which every salesman should ask himself now and again.

1 Do I know enough about the goods I am selling or the product I am handling to enable me to talk about them intelligently to any prospect?

2   Can I explain everything about my product so
    clearly that my prospect could, if necessary, resell
    it?
3   As no product is perfect, what is there about mine
    that a competitor could criticise?
4   Do I know the trade terms relating to the product?
    Do I know the trade terms of the principal busines-
    ses I call on?
5   Do I know enough about my product not to be
    afraid of any questions I may be asked about it?

That's a good checklist, and you will be well advised to
run through these points once every three months.

Obtaining information

There is a mine of information awaiting the salesman
who will trouble to dig for it.

Head office

What do his company's sales executives know of
a customer? What information is there in company
files?

Direct selling

The speciality salesman making anything from ten to
twenty calls a day cannot check prospective customers
with head office. But local traders will often talk about
their neighbours.
    Even if a salesman is unsuccessful at a call, he can
still ask for information. He may say:
    'Can you tell me the name of the owner of the shop
opposite?'
    'Has she been there long?'

'What kind of a woman is she?'
'Has she a partner?'
The answers will help that salesman to make a good approach when calling on these merchants.

Newspapers

A salesman selling high-priced equipment should read the City pages. He will learn of new developments, of the background of top executives, and plans for expansion. In company reports he will find further information to help him talk in terms of the customers' interests.

Salesmen selling to smaller traders should read the local newspapers. There may be nothing useful in them for twenty-five weeks out of twenty-six, but on the twenty-sixth week there may be something that will indicate a sales opportunity. A shopkeeper is always pleased when a representative mentions his advertisements in the *Watling Gazette*, or what the editor of the *Blankton Star* wrote about his special window display; or makes a reference to his speech at the opening of an old peoples' home.

Some salesmen do better than others because they take their jobs more seriously. It is time-consuming to read local newspapers, but such time spent in preparation for an order is always worthwhile.

Trade magazines, too, can help salesmen to keep up to date in many aspects of their job. Such publications are a must for salesmen.

Directories

At our offices details of new publications with up-to-date information about companies and company directors are received regularly. No salesman could be expected to buy these sets of directories, but they are nearly always available at local libraries. In directories you can find:

(a) Names of directors of companies.
(b) Names and addresses of companies within a group.
(c) Products manufactured or sold by a division of an organisation.
(d) Capital structure.
(e) Number of employees.

Observation

Observation plays a part in pre-planning. A change of name on a shop's fascia, or a good window display, can help a salesman to surmount the first hurdle of the approach. The store buyer's preferences may be seen in the range of goods in the window. It might be too late to obtain a contract when it is seen that a site is being levelled for a new building, but there could still be opportunities with the building director or developer. The salesman can learn something from the type of car parked outside an office or shop, from the decor of a waiting-room – from the letter-headings of a company's stationery – from advertising campaigns – from the general staff atmosphere...

Other salesmen

Salesmen are by nature talkative. Analytical chemists or accountants do not talk a great deal about their work, but salesmen are always ready to describe victories or defeats. Listeners, we know, can always learn something, and other salesmen can be surprisingly helpful. Many a useful hint has been picked up from their idle chatter at the end of the day. They will refer to the peculiarities of customers, the ease with which a receptionist can be outmanoeuvred, the new machinery being installed in a certain factory, a new shop being opened...

No honourable salesman would get information from a competitor who might be ignorant of his reasons for asking, but representatives selling non-competitive goods have much to teach. A salesman selling office machinery may have noticed that new partitioning is needed in an office. A book salesman may know of a store's new department for cosmetics.

Make friends with other salesmen. They can be good friends to you.

The planners

Salesmen can be placed roughly (very roughly) in three categories: (a) the meticulous planner, (b) the constant planner, and (c) the semi-planner. Even the most unprofessional salesman will do *some* pre-call planning – if it is only to give thought to the name of the buyer he is calling on, or where he should park his car.

The *meticulous planner*, however, plans carefully each evening. First, he completes his report, then enters the details from it on to a card-index system. Next he considers his work for the following day. What time should he spend telephoning to get appointments, or, if his appointments are already made, how long should he spend with each buyer? What are their needs? And so on...

The *constant planner* is nearly always an enthusiast, deeply concerned with every aspect of his job. He is continually planning – thinking ahead. He does not necessarily set aside a special time for planning, because he is always planning – always jotting down notes.

Unfortunately, many a salesman is a *semi-planner*, believing that he can *play it by ear*. He never bothers to

keep a card-index system, relying on his memory to
bring back to his mind details of customers' requirements, names of decision-influencers. . .

An example of the difference between the *meticulous
planner* and the *semi-planner* is that the first will always
carry with him coins or a card, for use in a public
telephone. The *semi-planner* would never dream of
checking whether he had the coins in his pocket each
morning, and sometimes has to make excuses to his
customer – 'I'm so sorry I'm late but my car broke
down and I didn't have a coin for the 'phone box.
Believe it or not I couldn't find a single passer-by who
had change'.

The *semi-planner* is a muddler, who only does well if
he is an outstandingly good salesman.

Weekly planning

A name sometimes given to weekly planning is
armchair planning. This means taking time off to
deliberate and work out strategies for the week ahead.
Maybe it takes place when the family have gone to bed,
or before embarking on a Sunday picnic. Somehow
time has to be found, unless you are a constant planner.
But even the constant planner needs to set aside some
time to consider more carefully the notes he has made
during the week.

Daily planning

Although customer and prospect cards are checked at
weekends, it is wiser to study those applicable to the
following day's work each evening. Daily planning is in
the main a study of customers and prospective customers.
The salesman will want to be reminded:

1   What a company manufactures, if any new products

have been introduced, and if the company has made known any future plans.

2   If anything has been sold to that company previously, in which case details should be available.

If there has ever been any complaints about products or after-sales service.

If they can be supplied. It is not unusual for a salesman to take an order only to find that a stop has been put on that particular account, perhaps because payments are in arrears, or more usually because it has not been possible to get extra insurance cover against bad debts.

If the company is a prospective customer, which products will interest the buyer.

If there are any quotations outstanding, which competitors' products are they using.

3   Who has authority to buy, and who could influence a buying decision.

4   Facts about a buyer – his interests.

5   Details of points discussed at a previous call.

6   Opportunities for future business.

7   Buyers' main needs.

8   The main objective of the call.

9   The secondary objective.

Never risk losing a buyer's confidence by demonstrating with equipment which could be faulty. Rather put off the demonstration until perfect units are available. Similarly, a sales kit must be checked to be certain that there are no dog-eared or stained leaflets, indecipherable drawings, or out-of-date figures.

Sales literature and sales aids should always be placed in the briefcase in the same order. This enables the salesman to extract the appropriate leaflet or catalogue without looking away from the buyer.

The objective of sales planning is to be prepared for every

eventuality. Sales planning ensures that you give your buyer or prospective buyer the best possible service.

The salesman who appreciates the value of pre-planning obviates guesswork, and lays the ground for success at each call.

15 Getting the interview

Some salesmen have no problem in obtaining interviews. Others need special techniques to enable them to meet a prospective buyer.

Some buyers avoid seeing salesmen. The salesman calling regularly on retailers and wholesalers, where usually the buyer works in the shop or the stock room, will have little difficulty in talking directly with the one person who can place orders. With other buyers it can be different. It is the barrier that can cause the trouble.

The barrier can be a closed door with a commissionaire sitting outside and refusing to allow anyone in without permission, a typist sitting in an office, a receptionist who knows every ploy used by salesmen to worm their way into the boss's office. Alternatively, the barrier can be a telephonist who has been told never to put through a call to the boss unless it has first been vetted by his secretary; and that secretary can often be a most difficult barrier to overcome, for she knows the value of her boss's time.

If you have no problems in obtaining interviews, then you can skip this chapter. But a wait a minute! Does that always apply, 100 per cent? If it does, it could mean that a salesman is no longer looking for new business.

If you are selling *widgets*, which a buyer has sold for many years, he has to buy those *widgets* because they

are accessories included in his product. You will have
no trouble in meeting such a buyer directly.

But such customers can be lost. The buyer could
change, or switch to a competitor, so that the salesman
should really always be looking for new outlets – new
accounts for him to open.

Many salesmen seem to enjoy their ruts. They don't
even want to attempt to make new calls, because they
are happy with their current selling and buying situation. They meet their targets, but if others are meeting
targets also, why should one salesman be promoted
over another? Possibly the reason could be that one
salesman opens more new accounts than another; so it
is not unusual for a salesman having to make the
attempt to open a new account occasionally finding it
difficult to be seen by the person who is already
satisfied with a competitor's products.

This chapter is to help those who, even on occasion,
find it hard to get past that barrier.

Appointments by telephone

How can a salesman get the maximum number of
interviews? What are his alternatives?

He can call cold, or make appointments by telephone.

Even if he is given enquiries to follow up, he will,
more often than not, have to telephone for an appointment. Cold-calling, or prospecting, as it is sometimes
called, will always have its place in selling but it is usually a
fill-in for most salesmen.

Rather than waste time between appointments a
salesman will often call cold on any nearby prospect;
but prospecting as a planned system of working can be
very time-consuming. For example, there can be long
waits in reception areas until a buyer is disengaged.
Moreover, a full day's work may result in only two

good interviews. But telephoning in advance may enable a salesman to make four or five appointments in a day.

Preparation

Unless the telephone call is made on a routine basis by a salesman calling on his customers every few weeks or months, and these customers will set aside time to see the salesman, the basis of all telephone selling must be good preparation. There are several rules to follow, and one golden rule: *you must find out the prospect's name.*

Knowing the prospect's name will help you to handle his telephone operator, and by addressing the buyer by name you are able to bring immediate warmth to the relationship. When you telephone either a customer or a prospect, remember:

1 The names and telephone numbers of the calls you intend making should be listed in front of you, and of course pen and paper must always be available for making notes.

2 You must have the customer files or information cards, directories, brochures, etc. available. This allows you to anticipate the customer's or prospect's questions or objections to giving an interview.

   A customer may have a delivery complaint. A prospect may not have bought from you previously because he considered your prices too high. With this knowledge available to you, you can forestall his queries.

3 Your diary is invaluable to you. Whenever possible, you will suggest days and times for appointments to suit *your* convenience. Your aim must be to fill the day with appointments.

4 Make sure that you will not be disturbed while telephoning.

Now, are you ready?

Let us assume that your name is White, and that you are calling a production director, a Mr Dawson. Although you want to speak to him personally, you must *never* make a misleading statement to obtain your objective.

Making the call

Pick up the telephone, dial the number, and, when greeted by the telephone operator, ask to speak to Mr Dawson.

One of three things can happen:

(a) The operator will transfer you immediately to Mr Dawson and all will be well.
(b) The operator will ask your business.
(c) The operator may put you through to Mr Dawson's secretary.

To avoid the second or third alternative you must have an authoritative approach. 'Will you please tell Mr Dawson, your production manager, that John White is on the line for him. Thank you.'

The *John* personalises the approach.

Never use the designations Mr, Mrs, Ms or Miss.

The '*Thank you*' gives it a finality which does not invite any response. Unless the telephone operator has had special screening instructions regarding incoming calls, you will be put through to Mr Dawson.

Alternatively, the operator may ask you for further information, and you will answer simply, 'It is a business matter'. Don't add anything further. It is not a misleading statement, because it is a business matter (not a personal call), which you can discuss only with Mr Dawson, the production manager. It will show equal authority if you imply that you wish to discuss something of importance, for example, 'It is in connection with Mr Dawson's new factory production plans (output, forecast, pension plan, new hygiene regulations. . .)'

There is another excellent approach if a letter has been sent to the buyer in advance. Then you can say, 'It is with reference to the letter I wrote him. . .' If the operator has been instructed to insist on obtaining information from every caller asking for Mr Dawson, you must say, 'I'm sorry, but it is a very involved matter. I think it might be best if you put me through to Mr Dawson's secretary'.

Sometimes it is advisable when making appointments to ask for a secretary in the first place, but in the main it is better to ask for the executive concerned. The secretary may be away or out of her office, and in this event the operator may put you straight through to the person you want to contact. If you speak to the secretary, however, either by your own request or because the operator has instructions to put you through to her, you will then have the selling task of persuading her to make an appointment for you to see Mr Dawson. You will use such golden words as: '*I should like to ask your advice.* I want to see Mr. Dawson because. . .'

You won't win every time, but you will win far more often than you lose. In most cases you will therefore be able to speak to Mr Dawson.

And what do you say to him?

The hinge

This can be a letter which you or your company have written, an advertisement, a new product, a special claim that you can make for your product, or a reference from a friend or business associate.

Your approach should be, 'Mr Dawson, this is John White of the Bridgwater Machine Tool Company. Have you a moment to speak on the telephone?' This courteous request, 'Have you a moment. . .', is not laid down as a fixed rule, but it can be very effective. It relaxes the prospect, because you have only asked him for a moment of his time, and it shows a courtesy that is too often lacking in so many telephone calls. Whether you use this sentence or not, you must then repeat the prospect's name after giving him the name of your company.

Letter hinge

'Mr Dawson, did you receive my letter?'
'No, what was it about?'
'Mr Dawson, it was about your. . .'

Reference hinge

'Mr Dawson, we haven't met, but John Williams asked me to contact you. . .' You will then have to sell Mr Dawson on the idea that you are worth seeing.

Question hinge

When you haven't a hinge of any kind, ask a question: 'Mr Dawson, this is Norman Boon of the Bessing Group. Have you heard of our organisation?' Whether the answer is yes or no is immaterial, because it will take you smoothly into the main reason for your call.

The quick approach close

The buyer might be influenced by the name of your company, or interested in the product or service you are selling – or he may like the sound of your voice. It may even be that he is very busy and arrives at a quick decision. Whatever the reason, this form of approach does get appointments. This is how it is done.

You must speak with conviction in your voice, to create the impression that there cannot be a refusal. You say, 'Good morning Mrs Braid, this is Jack Adams of Halliday Publications. I should like to take up just five minutes of your time to tell you about our new journal for your industry, and its wonderful advertising pull. Would Wednesday morning or Wednesday afternoon be more convenient for me to call?'

This approach covers a lot of ground. It is brief, it asks for only a short interview, it states your business, and it closes.

Be special

A winning word to use in all approaches is *special* or *specially*: Mr Tattersall, I am calling you *specially* to tell you about. . .'; or 'Mr Lawson, there is a *special* reason why I should like to see you. . .'

Keep to the rules

Although the quick close will get you interviews, in many cases there will be a request for further information. Here are some points to remember:

(a) Time is not on your side, so keep the benefit short.
(b) You must not try to present a full sales offer.
(c) Keep the objective in mind: *to obtain an interview*.
(d) Use short sentences and understandable words.
(e) Be authoritative, but never talk down to the buyer.
(f) Don't try to be too clever. You have to persuade the prospect that you are a sincere person by the words you use, and by the tone of your voice.

(g) Have a reason for not giving full information over the telephone, e.g. samples to be shown, a model of a building to examine, figures to analyse, a drawing to discuss, or matters so personal that they should be discussed face to face.

The main benefit

You must stake your claim for an interview in a few compelling words:

1 'I'd like to show you a recent survey which. . .'
2 'You will want to consider six ideas for cutting down overheads in your offices. . .'
3 'We have designed a very unusual programme, which will be of great benefit to you. . .'
4 'The Mighty Midget computer is no larger than your desk pad. Knowing something of your company's activities, I'm sure you would find this of tremendous help for personal use. . .'
5 'You would want to handle the stitcher yourself, to see how well it works. . .'

Your aim is to intrigue the prospect, to interest him, so that he will want to hear more and will give you an interview.

The objections

What could his objections be? He could hardly object to your product or service, because you have only given him the barest outline. He could only object to your taking up his time at an interview.

He could answer: 'I'll see you.' Then all would be well. But he could also say 'Send me the information', 'Tell me now', or 'I'm too busy'.

There are several ways of tackling the request for further information:

(a) 'Mr Pomeroy, you would want to see proof of how a company has been able to increase production by up to 28 per cent. . .'

(b) 'What I want to talk to you about, Ms Gillespie, is the details of a new way in which you can protect your money, and beat inflation. Would next Tuesday morning at. . .?'

(c) 'Mr Cuffley, you demand a very fast delivery service. We can provide that at low cost, and you will want to examine this claim. It is for this reason that I am asking for the opportunity to meet you. May I call. . .?'

(d) 'I cannot advise you, Mrs Kincaid, until I know one or two things about your company. . .'

(e) 'You would need to look at our analysis forms, Mr Tucket, and I shall bring them with me. It will only take a few minutes. May I call on. . .?'

To the statement 'I am too busy' the salesman has several answers, according to what he is selling: 'That is why I am telephoning you Mr Jeffries, instead of calling, because I know you are so busy. You can make any time, to suit your own convenience. May I suggest some alternative dates. . .?'

Ego-building can also be a sound policy: 'Mr White, I have found that it is the busy people like you who are most interested. . .'

Another approach is to assume that the prospect is only encountering a temporary rush of business: 'Of course, Mrs Howell, I know how busy you are. I wasn't thinking of disturbing you today or tomorrow. Will you be able to see me on Thursday or Friday of next week?'

If you reach a point where you feel you are antagonising the prospect, then you must never shut the door to a future appointment. 'I'll call you again in a fortnight, Mr Barclay.'

If this doesn't work there is always one final request that you can make, one that is rarely refused: 'Mr Brittain, there are some times of the day when you are not so busy as others, although I appreciate that you can't specify them. When I am next near your offices, may I call on the offchance of seeing you?' He will nearly always agree, and this is noted in your cold-calling diary. Following that telephone call, after two or three visits at the most, you will find that you will see Mr Barclay.

The close

Tying up an appointment is different from locking up an order, when you can use any of the closes set out in the sales presentation. This is not possible when selling the interview. Nearly always therefore you should use the *alternative close* based on an appointment time.

Most salesmen suggest a time for a meeting on the hour or the half-hour. You can be different. Put forward 9.10 am or 3.50 pm. The very unexpected nature of this suggestion will often bring its own reward. But the main reason for using this technique is that many busy people make appointments on the hour or half-hour, some of which will last the full period, while others will be cut short. The odd time therefore will often appeal to the prospect whose appointments on the hour may leave him periods in between which are free. Another approach is to suggest a time band (2.30 to 3.30 perhaps).

Remember, you are only asking for a few minutes of his time, knowing that if you can interest him he will ask you to stay. The close can therefore be:

'Will Wednesday or Thursday suit you best, Mr Lovell?'

'Er – Wednesday.'

'Afternoon.'

'That's fine, Mr Lovell. Can you make it 2.10? Or would 4.50 be more convenient?'

'Ten past two would suit me.'

'Thank you, Mr Lovell. I shall look forward to being with you at ten past two on Wednesday.'

Conclusion

To succeed in obtaining more appointments by telephone you must:

1 Know your prospects and their business.
2 Have a definite reason for asking for the interview.
3 Have a planned approach.
4 Have a main benefit to stress the need for the appointment.
5 Be prepared to listen and never pounce. (It might be that the prospect is about to give you an interview when you interrupt.)
6 Smile when you talk on the telephone.
7 Talk a little more slowly than usual.
8 If not making headway, ask questions.
9 Sound enthusiastic. Your enthusiasm will vibrate over the wires and will do more than anything else to get that appointment for you.

The obtaining of appointments is a challenge to all salesmen – a challenge which, if accepted, can lead to a far greater volume of business.

Prospecting

If you can always get an appointment by sending through your card, then keep a good supply always available. If you have frequently called on a buyer, each time sending up your card and each time failing in your mission, you must work to a different plan.

The card might show the name of a company – Portland Tools Ltd, for example. A buyer glancing at it and being satisfied with his present suppliers will return it with the message, *nothing today*. But the salesman representing Portland Tool Ltd might have a special tool which would interest the buyer, and this information cannot be gleaned from the card.

Thousands of salesmen make thousands of abortive calls because they persist in using cards for the wrong reasons. Here is a technique which usually brings about interviews.

If a reception office is guarded by a telephonist, it is essential that you walk briskly up to the reception desk. If you have a hangdog look or appear ill at ease, you won't succeed even in the first part of your task, which is to convey a sense of the importance of your visit to the receptionist.

You smile and say, 'Good morning, will you please tell Mr Colquhoun that George Heyworth is here to see him'. Spell your name 'H-e-y-w-o-r-t-h' and then look away as if preoccupied with thoughts of great moment.

If you indicate that you expect to be questioned, she will invariably ask, 'What is your business?' In most cases, however, she will telephone Mr Colquhoun and tell him that Mr George Heyworth is in the waiting room to see him. Mr Colquhoun then has two choices: he can ask the telephonist, 'Will you please find out what he wants', or he can say, 'Tell him to come up and see me'.

If, however, in spite of your having looked away, the receptionist asks for information, you must give it. If, while telephoning Mr Colquhoun she says, 'Mr Colquhoun has asked the reason for your visit', you should try to answer Mr Colquhoun's question yourself. Reach for the telephone handpiece quite naturally, as if this question is expected, and say, 'May I have a word with him?' Now it is up to you to convince Mr Brown that he should see you.

Here are some rules to remember for obtaining more interviews:

1 Treat the receptionist with respect to obtain her co-operation.
2 Don't wait about too long. Your time is valuable. If someone is going to keep you waiting thirty or forty minutes, it may pay you better to make a call elsewhere.
3 If there is any reading matter relating to the firm's activities in the reception area, study it while you are waiting.
4 If you should have to wait a little while, don't keep worrying the receptionist.
5 When a secretary comes into the waiting room, don't forget to stand up, and she will appreciate words like, 'I should be grateful for your help', or 'I wonder if you can help me...?' Most people like helping others.

The final solution

If all else fails, be persistent in your calling if you believe that the buyer has the purchasing power to make your persistence worthwhile. Many times my secretary has said to me, 'You must see him, he's so nice and he's called so often'. She wins – and sometimes, the salesman wins, too.

Personal Advice from
Tack Managing Directors

You now know how Tack Training International evolved from the training of our own salesmen, and that the development of our air-conditioning division resulted from the chance meeting with an ex-salesman. Now for the story of how the determination of one person led us into the printing field.

South Western Printers

Now one of the leading printers in the South Wales area, this company owes a great deal of its success to the present managing director, Carlos Maza. Carlos began with us as an office boy. One of his main functions was to operate the duplicating machine – this was of course before the introduction of photocopiers. Our small duplicator was used for reproducing memoranda, bulletins, etc.

Very quickly Carlos requested a more advanced duplicator, which, he assured us, would allow us to carry out additional work, and save the cost of sending printing out. We said no, the cost was too high.

He must have visited us every day, on each occasion bringing additional benefits, and doing his best to persuade us that a new duplicator could be a great asset to the company.

We gave way.

It was not long before he was once more requesting a meeting to explain an even greater benefit which would accrue to the company, if we were to purchase an offset printing machine. Again I said no, and I won the day, because we didn't have the room for it in our head office premises in Victoria. However, he persevered and nagged, piling benefit on benefit, and when we took an additional factory in Kings Langley, Hertfordshire, he overcame the objection that we hadn't the room. He suggested that he should move to the factory and do our printing work from there.

Carlos was very quickly producing for us a house magazine and brochures, which had previously been printed for us by outside sources.

After a few years we again moved our manufacturing division to a much larger factory at Caerphilly, in South Wales. Carlos moved there and again, by dint of his determination, was able to obtain a large area for his print shop.

This, of course, meant that he began again demanding a larger and more sophisticated printing machine. To cut a long story short, Carlos argued his way to moving production eventually to larger premises, completely devoted to printing, and he has recently installed machines costing £1 million or more.

He was a technical man, but once he was in command of his print shop he then became a *salesman*, and achieved great success by his selling skills. Now of course he has a sales team working for him.

If you want to succeed beyond all expectations, leaving others far behind you, you can learn an important lesson from Carlos: *there is no substitute for enthusiastic determination – and a refusal to take no for an answer.*

Personnel hygiene services

There is a different lesson to be learned from our

entering the field of personnel hygiene (hand-dryers, towel-dispensers, vending machines, fly killers, and toilet hygiene).

Some years ago, not being satisfied with the sanitary towel disposal system being used in our offices, we sent for details of a bin which had been advertised, offering cleaning, collection, and replacement on a monthly basis.

The person who arrived to sell us the bin was the sales manager of the company concerned. After ordering the bins my secretary said to him, 'It was nice of you to call personally. I was rather expecting one of your salesmen'. He replied, 'Our units, as you know, are put out on a month's trial, so we don't need salesmen. They sell themselves'.

When she relayed this information to me, I remember saying, 'If they can succeed without employing any salesmen, imagine what we could achieve with our trained sales force!' And so it happened. Against intense competition we have become the leaders in this field.

The director who created our successful PHS organisation was at one time our financial director. But, unusually, he was a sales-minded accountant. It was his selling drive that did so much to help this company succeed, and now it employs some 300 sales women and 300 service women.

M. D. Bryan Newman tells me that a great lesson to be learned from the success of Personnel Hygiene Services is *always work systematically* – which, I suppose, is the way an accountant thinks about audits. Bryan said:

Our competitors rely so much on advertising. We don't advertise at all. We rely on a trained salesforce, and I keep driving home the necessity of working systematically – every shop, every office must be called upon, one after the other. No dodging around, no time wasted. This applies whether our women are calling on the largest stores or the giant conglomerates. There must be no missing of any opportunities to visit that special customer.

Never judge the buying abilities of a business by your own pocket, or by appearances. *Make the call* – then judge for yourself.

You will only know whether the prospect is worth calling on by calling – not by pre-judging. If you give everyone the opportunity to buy, you will find that the least likely prospect will often turn out to be one of the best buyers.

Our women also systematically cover local authorities, hospitals, restaurants, and hairdressers, but never out of sequence – always in a logical order, to save travelling time. This applies, whether you have to see chairmen, managing directors, or those who buy for the largest supermarket chains. If you work systematically, five days a week, you will achieve greater success.

To my mind a successful salesman will depend on the number of effective calls he can make each day.

So many salesmen, even the brilliant ones, never work to 100 per cent of their capacity, because they don't work systematically, starting early in the morning and finishing late in the evening.

That's excellent advice from Bryan Newman, who has built such a successful company.

PHS (Pest Control Division)

When Personnel Hygiene Services decided to enter the field of pest control, there was one problem: Rentokil were highly successful in that field.

There is an old adage which goes something like this: A small company cannot compete with a large company and become large itself, unless it has something different to offer – or unless, by some magical means, it can produce goods of equal quality at much lower prices. Obviously, we could not offer a very much different service. What we could offer, however, were better marketing and selling skills.

David Willcox, the managing director of this division, says, 'It was sales training that helped us to overcome competition, in spite of our prices often being higher than those of our competitors. Only good training can help a salesman to overcome such a disadvantage, and can turn that disadvantage of price into an advantage'.

Remember, PHS training is based on everything you are reading in this book. Such training can succeed against even the stiffest opposition.

Tack Management Consultants

Careful listening brought this company into existence. A salesman told me that he had lost an order because a competitor had offered first to send in consultants to define a need. Three months after meeting that salesman, Tack Management Consultants came into existence.

Here is a message from Tom Trager, managing director of this company.

Having carried out many sales audits during my career as a management consultant, I have often pondered the eternal question: *what makes a star salesman?*

Of course star salesmen are more energetic, persistent, resilient, and ambitious than the average performer. Yet there is another ingredient, a yeast, which makes them rise faster than their colleagues. I think this yeast is *perception*, a quality which characterises a good management consultant.

Almost all consultancy assignments demand a rapid understanding of the client company's operations. There are only three ways to get this information: (a) reading reports, (b) interviewing staff, and (c) interviewing suppliers or customers.

A client will not expect the consultant to know minute details about his company in the first few days. During this period he will be tolerant of the consultant's misconceptions or incorrect assumptions. After a week, though, the consultant cannot afford to ask basic questions about the product or the organisation; he or she will be expected to have a thorough understanding. Working fast and accurately needs perception, deciding what is important and has to be remembered, and discarding the trivial.

A star salesman whom I once assessed told me that the premises' manager of a large head office always gave the impression to visiting salesmen that he was the sole buyer of supplies for photocopying equipment in that building. On one of his regular sales calls the salesman was scanning the staff newspaper, which was displayed in the reception area, when he noticed a photograph of the manager of the printing department standing proudly next to two large new photocopiers. The salesman began to question the accepted belief that the premises' manager was the sole buyer. A few discreet enquiries enabled him to discover that the manager of the printing department was responsible for all purchases in his department. A meeting was arranged, and eventually an order was obtained.

A star salesman has to be a good interviewer, just

like a skilled consultant. The art of good interviewing comprises:

1 Gaining the interviewee's confidence.
2 Letting the interviewee do the talking.
3 Keeping to the point.
4 Extracting the most relevant information in the limited time available.
5 Being alert for hints, tips, leads, that indicate there could be opportunities.

Gaining the respondent's confidence depends on being confident and authoritative oneself. Obviously appearance and the ability to communicate clearly are pre-requisites. Pre-planning and preparation are vital – knowing in advance exactly what you are going to ask, avoiding silences, or fumbling for a list of questions or a prop until you know you have the buyer's attention. The buyer has to be encouraged to talk about the market, his products, and his problems. Useful information can slip out, which could be to your advantage.

Direct, probing questions are needed by salesmen, as well as consultants. For example, many salesmen plough the same furrow on each sales call, and fail to find out anything new or look for new opportunities. I once carried out a sales audit for a company selling audio-visual services to exhibition-stand organisers. The salesman regularly visited a large government authority, and always went to sell to the promotions' department, whose function was to organise exhibition stands. He had excellent relations with the buyer, and was frequently praised by his area manager for the orders he generated from this customer; yet he never thought to ask whether there were other departments which might use his product. All he need have done was to ask his contact the direct question, namely, what other advertising, public relations, or communications activities the authority was engaged in. We asked this question at the end of a sales call, and learned that:

(a) The corporate planners had to commission films and displays for investors to keep them informed of progress, and future developments.
(b) The public relations department was a major buyer, campaigning regularly to allay the public's fears about the safety of the industry.
(c) The information officer's job was to communicate with schools, and therefore he commissioned educational films.

These departments were located in different buildings, and each had its favourite supplier, but there is no doubt that a successful salesman would have gained orders. There is after all nothing better than a glowing reference from another department in a large organisation to open the door to an order.

Consultancy and selling also share the common feature of collecting information, analysing it, and drawing pertinent actionable information. Information about competitors is vital in maintaining market share. Salesmen have to be alert and aware to recognise the significance of a competitor's actions. To react too quickly to an isolated item of information may result in a wild-goose chase.

I recall the case of a company which received reports from a thermometer salesman that many customers, including a major account, were going to reduce purchases of mercury and spirit thermometers in favour of the digital variety. This naturally caused considerable alarm, since the company's factory was solely dedicated to manufacturing traditional thermometers. After some investigation at senior level it was learned that only the one account had made such a statement, and its plan was simply to test digital products. The salesman had jumped to the wrong conclusions from insufficient evidence. Consultants and salesmen cannot afford to make such generalisations, which undermine confidence and leads to their managers questioning their judgement.

All the attributes I describe here are connected with perception – being sensitive to the customer's needs, being aware of the broader implications of a statement, being alert to other opportunities by not focusing exclusively on one target.

Finally, always be sure of having all the facts before reaching any conclusions and giving advice to your managers.

Tack management training

Wherever I travel, the Far East, Middle East, South Africa, Canada, the USA, and whenever I meet an executive and my name is mentioned the immediate response is, 'Are you the Alfred Tack of the Sales Training Company?' That is the reputation we have built up over the years.

Today the value of bookings for management-training courses is some 40 per cent of our turnover, and it is a rising figure. This success is due largely to the drive of Eric Pillinger, managing director of our training division.

Among the successful courses he has introduced was one on time management – how to plan your time successfully, so important to the salesman. This is the advice he has to give you on the subject:

Your time is very expensive, and so you must make sure that you use it to the best effect. It isn't just your salary, pension, insurance, etc., it is your car, your expenses, your sales literature, and all the other direct expenses, as well as the indirect costs of recruiting, training, and administration. The cost of wasted time is also the cost of lost sales opportunities or business lost to competitors.

A good starting point is to remember the principles of selling by objectives – that simple planning discipline which helps you to meet your targets. You identify overall performance objectives by which you will be judged (e.g. total sales, sales within product groups, new accounts opened, average order value). You then break these down into quarterly/monthly/ weekly targets. Finally, you plan clear objectives for each client contact – by telephone, letter, or face to face. Selling by objectives is the first step in managing your time, because it identifies your priorities and the 'critical activities' you must undertake to achieve the right results.

So the main guideline is *to spend your time where it counts most*. This may sound obvious, but many of us kid ourselves into thinking that we do this, when really we are spending our time where it is easiest or most enjoyable! You must strike the right balance between contacting potential customers, closing new business, and developing and protecting existing accounts. This is called 'working to priorities'.

To be fully cost-effective you need to maximise total face-to-face selling time (or personal telephone contact time where this is an alternative). This in turn means minimising travelling time and unproductive or wasted time, and ensuring that you are spending your personal selling time productively. Allocate the number of calls and the amount of time devoted to clients and prospects in direct proportion to their actual or potential business volume. A popular grading system is:

A – large clients/prospects.
B – medium clients/prospects.

C – small but expanding.
D – small but declining.

Ensure that the As and Bs receive most of your attention, but that the Cs and Ds are not completely neglected. Remember that the total time you devote is made up of the number of contacts and the average duration of those contacts. You must also spend your time with the right people, who can either be decision-makers or decision-influencers, or a combination of the two. Do not waste much time with those who have neither authority nor influence, but, equally, you must never make enemies of them by ignoring them completely.

Deciding how much time to spend on each client or prospect is the first step. Then you have to decide how and where to contact them. Contact by telephone and/or mail is never as good as a personal visit. But it is better than nothing, and can be an efficient way of cutting down the total amount of personal selling time needed, especially with Cs and Ds. But you need a good territory planning technique for fitting in as many personal calls as possible, and also leaving you enough flexibility to respond to urgent requests. Because territories differ so much in size, layout, and client density, there is no single technique that works for everyone – you have to work out one which suits your circumstances.

Before you can do that you have to be well organised in yourself. You need the right equipment and paperwork. No one can say exactly what is best for you, but it must be manageable by you, suited to your style of work and your working locations, (e.g. at home, in the office, out in your car, in hotels, on aeroplanes...) and cost-effective for your company (e.g. if everyone had portable computers and mobile telephones, then everyone would probably be more efficient, but the cost to the company could be much greater than the value of the extra efficiency).

Write everything down. Don't rely on your memory, because everyone's gets worse without their realising it, as they get older. Have an appropriate diary for listing all your 'fixed' tasks, i.e. appointments or other activities to be done at a certain date or time; also make sure you have a task list for all your outstanding 'floating' tasks, which have to be done but not at any specific time. It is often these tasks, such as identifying new potential accounts, which will give you the big long-term pay-off, but are easily overlooked.

A good tip is also to work through your list in reverse order of liking, first doing the things that you hate most, and leaving until last the jobs you enjoy doing. This is an excellent way of avoiding procrastination, and somehow or other you always find time to fit in your favourite tasks! Another hint for using potentially wasted time is to identify 'time-fillers' – small jobs that can be done in the five minutes between meetings in the office, the ten minutes you are kept waiting in customers' reception areas, or the rather more minutes of waiting time in airports or stations (or traffic jams). Have these time-fillers readily to hand, and fit them into small time gaps during the day, so that you can use longer time gaps, e.g. half an hour at your desk early in the morning, before leaving for your first call, to fit in larger jobs needing periods of unbroken concentration.

How about the time you spend in your car? Journey planning is easy in theory but difficult in practice. Try to plan your calls and your travel so as to minimise time and mileage and maximise customer contact. Try to make your customers fit in with you as far as possible. Customer orientation is all very well, but when you hear of sales people driving all day to meet one C or D customer, just because 'he phoned and asked me to call in and see him', you think maybe it can be taken too far. It is often hard to arrange appointments in a chronologically and geographically convenient way, but only 'amateur' salespeople opt for the line of least resistance rather than taking the line of most productivity.

Delegation is another time-honoured method of saving time. Is there some routine function which you could ask one of your sales office staff to do for you? Are you spending time doing something which a typist could do equally well, at lower cost? You can even consider delegating something to your manager or your spouse. The scope for delegation varies, but it does link in with another very important time-management principle – time investment. Can you invest time today to save time tomorrow, next week, or next year? For instance, could you work out a number of standard pages or paragraphs, so that it is easy to write apparently 'tailor-made' letters or proposals? Should you spend a few hours reorganising your records or files, to save wasted time searching for information? Or – and this is where it relates to delegation – should you invest time in training others, or indeed yourself, to increase their skills and help you with your workload? Most of us never make the time to make the investments which would save us time.

Old habits die hard, but new habits can improve efficiency. Do you have efficient routines for ensuring that you do the less exciting parts of your job on time, and relatively painlessly? Try having a certain time of the week when you complete your routine paperwork. Try and make it a habit to write up your records immediately after each call, or at the end of each day. Fill up with petrol regularly at the start or end of the day, to save time during the working day itself. Maybe you should make it a discipline to do a little bit of administrative work before leaving for your first call each morning, or to read your trade journals during lunch breaks or coffee breaks. Making a habit of something, or fixing a routine, saves time and energy and reduces the self-discipline required to do what we know we ought to be doing anyway.

Have you tried 'floating start times' for appointments? Instead of fixing a definite time – 'I'll be with you at 3 pm' – try asking customers if you can arrive during a certain time band, e.g. 'May I come sometime between 2.30 and 3.30?' The worst they can say is 'No', and surprisingly often they will agree. This gives you much more flexibility. You don't have to leave a safety margin in your travel schedule, and you may be able to fit in an extra visit each day if you use this system effectively. If nothing else, it means less apologising for being late because of traffic hold-ups! In addition, how about fixing customer meetings for unusual times – very early in the morning, late at night, during lunch hours, or at weekends? Customers will rarely be insulted by such requests – generally just the opposite, because it shows your dedication. How much such dedication you are prepared to show is your decision alone.

What about technology? Nothing stands still, but do not go for 'hi-tech' for its own sake. It must be cost-effective, and most salespeople are limited here by what their companies are prepared to spend. But all of us can now afford hand-held computers or 'organisers' out of our own pocket, if necessary. Whether it is better to use one of these or a simple combination of diary and card index depends on you and your preferences. Many salespeople now buy their own word processors or home computers, out of personal or family interest, and then use them for

work as well. It may or may not make you more
efficient, but it is always worth considering. But quite
apart from electronics, do you carry equipment for
all possible contingencies with you in your car?
Coins, 'phone cards, tool kit, de-icer, jump leads,
tow rope, stamps, stationery, stapler, etc?' Always
take some customer details with you for 'contingency'
calls, if you have a cancelled appointment or a meeting
which is shorter than expected.

But at the end of the day (or the end of the year for
many of us) what will have the greatest effect on
results is not technology, equipment, territory plans,
or computer print-outs, it is our own skill and knowledge. The best use of our time is to learn about our
product or service and our organisation; to learn how
to analyse our customers' needs, and to learn how to
bring the two together in a skilful and professional
way. Remember that if your ability level is high
and your effort level is high, your only serious time-
management problems will be caused by an excess of
orders, and probably also an excess of income. Can
there be such a problem?

Advice from Denmark

Thirty years ago Knud Bagger sought our concession
for Denmark. We turned him down because of lack of
finance on his part. Then he mortgaged his home and
applied again, for us to reconsider our decision.

Thank goodness we did!

By his drive, ability, and integrity, his company has
become the leading training organisation of its kind in
Denmark. Tack there is a household name, due to
Knud's efforts, and the brilliant team of directors/
instructors he has built around him.

In paying tribute to him, we are also paying tribute to

all those overseas who have played such a big part in building the name of Tack throughout the world.

Here is some good advice from Knud:

Let us make the following supposition: you are driving to meet your next customer when the time for the weather forecast on the radio approaches. It interests you, because you want to know what the weather is going to be like the following day, when you have to make a long journey to another area. You turn on the car radio.

The announcer is as ambiguous as ever, claiming sunshine here, rain there, and varying temperatures everywhere. Despite the fact that you have been listening carefully, you are still unclear as to what the weather is going to be like the following day. Later that evening, after watching the news on TV, a weather forecast map flashes onto the screen and, in a moment, tomorrow's weather is imprinted on your mind.

May I ask you, when you visit a customer, do you function like the radio or TV? There is no doubt that your customer's brain functions like yours does. He can miss, misunderstand, or forget your words; but that would never happen if you used *visuals*.

Forgive me for quoting once more, that gem from China: *one picture is worth a thousand words*. Yet salesmen regularly forget that truth from bygone days. They do not use visuals enough. They do not use them in the right order. They do not use them as a memory aid. They do not therefore use them to strengthen their presentation.

The Tack ABC sequence is so logical, and the Tack selling sentence technique will keep a salesman on track for the complete presentation. Visual aids not only reinforce the ABC of selling, but allied to the selling sentence technique, they ensure that no benefit will be forgotten.

Right from the approach, you should consider what you can use to illustrate and substantiate benefits.

After the approach and interest stage it is essential to present visual material to create confidence.

Most buyers are sceptical about offers made to them. It would indeed be irresponsible of them not to question a product's quality and the supplier's integrity. That is why visuals are so important to support the words you use. The fact that you represent a first-class company with excellent products is not necessarily proven by words alone. The buyer needs more confirmation, because competitors do their best to undermine his faith in you.

What are your confidence-creators? You should seek them out – a letter from a satisfied customer, an official approval, a photograph of quality control in action, a report of your company's activities, a fleet of service vans, a picture of research laboratories – or simply an outstandingly good brochure, printed on high-class paper, well designed, perfectly laid out, and still in its pristine glory. . . That visual aid alone can help to create confidence, while a dog-eared leaflet will engender a loss of belief in the quality of a company's offer.

In Denmark we tell delegates at our courses that selling can be hard or easy, and it can be made so much easier if use is made of what we call *the sales sequence visual aid.*

This can be several aids put together – brochures, leaflets, photographs, samples – but the essential factor is that they must all be placed in the salesman's case in logical order. After a call has been made, there should be an inspection of the case, to ensure that they are still in the right order, ready for the next call.

Every one of the visuals shown will be equivalent to so many half heard spoken words.

Some sales people have told me that they have no visuals, but this is no hindrance to creativity. Even the smallest businesses today usually have a photo-copier. If you don't have a good visual aid, then use a photocopier to paint pictures of your sequence.

A Polaroid camera may also be used in the making of first-class visual aids. Your objective is to try to match every benefit with such an aid.

In the 1980s a new concept, developed in the USA in the 1970s, reached Europe and Scandinavia. It was called *body language*.

Unfortunately all it did was to cause many sales-people to concentrate on their body language, and their act became hesitant and unnatural. But if you let your visuals do the main work for you, you will become relaxed and enthusiastic, and you can forget about your *body language*!

Never expect a buyer to read from your brochure or leaflet. He may look interested, but he is not.

Point out to him emphatically each benefit, and read it through to him. Then his eyes will move to the photograph or drawings, and this will mean that you are letting your visual aids do your selling for you.

Tack training overseas

Our training courses are now available in forty-four countries. We grant concessions to associate com-panies; and all their chief executives, together with their instructors, attend indoctrination and refresher training in London.

The managing director of Tack Training Overseas is Bill Stanley. In his early days he was a great success as an instructor for Tack in Eire. He is now in demand world-wide, for his exceptional skills as a trainer and public speaker.

He took over Tack Training Overseas some 20 years ago, and although he hates flying, he spends most of his time flying to faraway places. He built our overseas division to leadership in this field. Here is some good advice from him:

Only a Yorkshireman can sell in Yorkshire. This was one of the first pieces of information given me on my entry into the selling environment in England – it had a most familiar ring!

So many times during my previous selling career in Ireland I had heard the sayings, *Only a Corkman can sell in Cork* and *Only a Dublinman can sell in Dublin*. In each case it only took a very few client calls to disprove these old myths. Without being a native of any of these areas I found it just as easy to sell in Cork as in Dublin – and indeed as in Yorkshire! Within a short time of taking up residence in the United Kingdom I found myself selling on the international scene, and, like an echo from the past, I heard *Only a German can sell in Germany, Only an American can sell in the USA* ... Once again it needed very few client calls in these areas, and indeed in the Middle and Far East, throughout Europe, and in Latin America, to discover that the thinking was just as wrong as when I had heard it applied to Dublin, Cork, or Yorkshire.

Why is it that so many people, sometimes quite experienced sales and marketing people, feel that it takes a different kind of technique to sell in each of the multiplicity of markets represented around the world? Are they saying that human beings are basically different because they live on one side or the other of a national border? Are they saying that customers have different needs? Are they saying that people respond to different motivations because they happen to be French, German, Dutch, or Indonesian rather than Canadian, Australian, or Scandinavian? Or are they saying that people of different nationalities have different hopes and aspirations?

Both as a salesman and sales trainer of many years' experience, I have to say that I cannot find these great differences which are supposed to exist – differences which mean that a native of one country or area cannot sell quite happily in a different environment. Experience has shown me that a good salesman is able to sell wherever he may find himself, provided he has a product which is value for money, and he has the backing of good sound training. Of course there are Germans who cannot sell in the UK, there are Japanese who cannot sell in the USA – indeed, as there are Englishmen who cannot sell in Central Europe or Latin America – but then these people are often unsuccessful in their home countries! Their inability to sell has nothing to do with the location in which they find themselves; a dedicated salesman, committed to his product, will sell anywhere, where there is a market, *provided* he takes account of certain basic and perhaps rather obvious factors.

First, he should not allow himself to develop a negative mental attitude simply because he has heard that *only a Yorkshireman can sell in Yorkshire.* Rather he must develop positive attitudes, because it *is* really all a question of attitudes. He must, first, accept that people are basically the same, regardless of where you find them. Populations throughout the world all have the same hopes and fears, frustrations and hostilities – and above all the same motivations. Customers, wherever we may meet them, want to have comfortable homes, give their families a good life, enjoy their leisure time free of doubts and worries, and of course to buy the best for their companies. If a salesman, well-trained in every way, keeps these points in mind, he is already three-quarters of the way towards achieving his selling objectives.

Of course the salesman must be aware that there *are* certain differences – ideological, political, religious, in various areas of the world – and even superstitions, which we must take account of. For instance, I could find myself discussing a training programme in 'Effective Supervision' with various production managers: the production manager in Canada will accept that one of his supervisors will have difficulty with operators who may be resistant to change, who do not know the reason for a decision, or who feel insecure in their jobs; and the production manager in some Third World country, or perhaps a country where the population is mainly of Chinese ethnic origin, will believe that productivity is low because there is a ghost under the machine. He *knows* that there is a ghost under the machine! This is perhaps a rather extreme example, but the salesman who is not aware of such factors, and prepared to take account of them, will obviously stand much less chance of success.

There are many other, perhaps rather less dramatic, examples of national differences that salesmen need to take account of, though they will in no way necessarily give rise to differences in the selling techniques employed in influencing the customer. As an example, in some parts of the world a higher degree of formality is required than in others. In the USA it is 'Bill, Bert, and Elmer' immediately on meeting. In Germany or Holland it might be better to observe the formalities rather longer. In the Middle East it is unwise to hand over a sales aid with the left hand; this may make life difficult for the naturally left-handed salesman, like me, but it would be considered rank bad manners by my clients in

Saudi Arabia. The enthusiastic salesman – and I find
no greater joy than seeing an enthusiastic salesman in
action – may punch his fist into the palm of his hand
to give emphasis or show pleasure, a gesture which
would be gravely misinterpreted in parts of the Far
East. Even the reflective flicking of the earlobe with
a forefinger could result in the salesman receiving a
punch on the nose, if he were selling in Rome!

BUT THE SELLING TECHNIQUES HE WILL
EMPLOY REMAIN THE SAME.

A high degree of tact is always required. Part of
this tact includes allowing the customer to 'save face'.
This is an expression which we always feel somehow
applies only to the Far East – and certainly, when we
sell in that part of the world, it would be very unwise
of us if, wherever necessary, we did not allow the
customer to save his face. However, I have had to do
exactly the same in Yorkshire *and* in Europe, *and* in
North and South America!

It is important, too, wherever we may meet
people, to look for opportunities to praise them,
their background, their company, their operations,
provided, of course, that this is justified. Praise
where praise can be honestly and justifiably given. I
do not know any part of the world where people do
not respond positively to it.

One of the attributes recognised in every corner of
the globe is true courtesy. I do not mean by this the
normal *please* and *thank you* of civilised living, but
more showing that we are prepared to fit in with
other nations' codes of behaviour, and to accept their
traditions and what to us may seem to be idiosyncra-
sies. Before I began to sell on the international
scene, I would sometimes read about something
happening in another country which sounded rather
peculiar to me – perhaps even very odd. However,
the more I visit various countries around the world,

the more I realise that what each country does within its own borders generally seems to be right for that country. It may seem unusual, but upon examination I usually find there is good reasoning behind behaviour which to me at first seemed unexpected, to say the least.

There is one personal characteristic, already mentioned in this book, but which cannot be too often repeated: Every salesman *must* project enthusiasm, which is always responded to by buyers in the same way, regardless of nationality, regardless of where they may be located round the world. People of all nations respond to it, they warm to it, they are influenced by it. It is very difficult for a customer to reject either the salesman or his message if that salesman is enthusiastic about his products, enthusiastic about his services, enthusiastic about his customers and their needs, enthusiastic about his company, and enthusiastic about benefiting the buyer.

The individual salesman must never be shy, embarrassed, or apprehensive about going into the international scene. He will find that his clients will respond to him in very much the same way as his clients respond to his influence at home. In other words, *selling is people – wherever you may find them*!

Nu-Aire Ltd

Salesmen selling technical products are sometimes of the opinion that their form of selling is difficult.

It isn't!

I asked Brian Moss, chief executive of Nu-Aire Ltd, a company employing very highly skilled technical salesmen, to give me his views. Here they are:

The basics of selling never vary, irrespective of whether you are selling baked beans or tractors. A salesman must have the right mental attitude, must most certainly pre-plan, must understand buyer motivation, and must prepare the best possible presentation, including all possible benefits – the presentation must appeal to the managing director, chief engineer, or draughtsman.

Naturally a salesman must have the ability to negotiate and close orders, although the closing is usually on a step by step procedure, which may be spread over many months.

Technical salesmen often do not tailor their presentation, however, to match selling opportunities. They translate product features into benefits in so generous a manner that the prospect doesn't perceive them as being of benefit to him.

The cure is for the technical salesman to be more aware of what is going on around him in the prospects' premises, aware of the plant and processes in the factories, drawings and models which may be shown to him, or at which he may only be able to get a passing glance. He must be aware of the actions of people, which may lead to other informative technical aspects of products. He can then really talk in terms of customer interest.

My next point is that a salesman is so often keen to show his own technical knowledge that he sometimes doesn't listen to what the prospect is saying, while exhausting his own arsenal of product specification clauses.

So, summed up, my hints to technical salesmen are:

1 Be observant. Learn about your prospect by conscientiously gleaning visual and oral information from the activities around you.

2 Do not bother your prospect with indigestible product facts.

3 Ask questions. Interrogate your prospects courteously about technical problems.

4 Personalise benefits. Your prospect must understand that *his* needs can be satisfied by *your* offer.

You will see from the above that all this advice does apply to salesmanship in general, but must be emphasised to the technical salesman.

There are two more points:

5 Be sure the prospect understands the technical jargon used in your factory.

6 Never, never give the impression that, because of your education, training, and well-earned degree, you are cleverer than the prospect. Seek his advice whenever possible, and so build up *his* importance.

The professional

There is all the difference in the world between the amateur and the professional. The difference is most marked in salesmanship:

1   The amateur salesman blames his territory for lack of sales. The professional blames himself.
2   The amateur tells a sales story. The professional lives the sales story.
3   The amateur, when worried, chases orders and high spots his territory. The professional, if worried, works his territory more systematically than ever.
4   The amateur takes the first 'No' as final. The professional accepts the first 'No' as a challenge, and sells all the harder.
5   The amateur says, 'I can't tackle this type of prospect' or 'I don't like calling on that type of trade'. The professional makes no distinctions.
6   The amateur talks about his wonderful products. The professional talks about the splendid business the prospect has and how he can make it even more profitable.
7   The amateur uses 'I' too often. The professional prefers 'You'.
8   The amateur always thinks money is short, even during boom times. The professional knows that when he creates the want the money is generally available.

9   The amateur believes it is calls that count. The professional knows that it is the effort he makes at every call which really matters.

10   The amateur sometimes neglects his appearance. The professional always takes pride in his clothes.

11   The amateur is ever ready to share the customers' pessimistic talk. The professional is always optimistic.

12   The amateur is always price-conscious. The professional only thinks of values.

13   The amateur lacks confidence and never really expects to get an order. The professional is always confident, and expects the order at every call.

Check up on yourself. Are you an amateur salesman, or a *professional salesman*?

Appendix
Specimen Offer Analysis
Sheets

1 PLASTIC-COATED STEEL SHEET FOR FABRICATION

Features	Benefits	'You appeal'
The sheet has a 200 micron PVC coating with a weathergrain effect	1 Provides long life to steelwork up to 45 years	You'll not need to worry about corrosion problems and customer complaints
	2 Requires little maintenance to achieve longevity	You can forget about constant overpainting to maintain appearance
	3 No preparation of sheets required	You can forget about paintshop costs and problems
	4 It is scratch-resistant	You can be sure that on-site handling problems and damage can be minimised
	5 Coating is malleable and can be bent back on itself	You will have no problems in forming the materials in your present forming machines

Features	Benefits	'You appeal'
The sheet has hot dipped galvanised substrate of 275 grammes zinc coat	1 Minimises corrosion problems	You will be able to satisfy the most stringent criteria and corrosion protection and obtain more business
	2 Zinc coating gives greater edge protection	You have no losses when cutting the material into smaller sheets
	3 It can be bent as required with no effect upon the zinc coating protection	You reduce your reject rate
	4 Zinc coating does not crack during forming	You can be assured that no outward rusting will occur
	5 Has distinctive advantages over the post painting of mild steels	You eliminate the cost of several coats of paint protection
	6 Has all the advantages of British steel technical back up	You can offer the latest coating technology to your customers

Sheet can be supplied from stock at any specified size to tolerances of 7.00 mm	1	Your company will receive materials cut to the tightest tolerances	You reduce machine time in production
	2	Materials are guaranteed for adherence to squareness	You know that the material will fit into your presses
	3	Your stocks can be reduced	Your costs are reduced and more space made available for you to use for other purposes
Small flexible company	1	All orders receive personal attention irrespective of size	You know that your order can be progressed immediately
	2	Able to react quickly to orders	You do not lose production, 'waiting for delivery'
	3	Close communication between departments	Your order will not be lost or delayed in the system
	4	No remote head office	You are able to speak to the person responsible for handling your order without having to go through intermediaries

Features		Benefits	'You appeal'
Largest approved stockist of OSC-coated products	1	Largest range of stocks of all coated steels	You do not waste time phoning several suppliers
	2	Large enough to be able to pass on the benefits of purchasing power	Your costs are reduced
	3	Large enough to be able to offer the best back-up available	Your company receives the full attention of OSC technical back up
	4	You are dealing with a company in the forefront of technological advancement in coated products	Your company can compete with the latest knowledge of up-to-date coatings
	5	Company personnel have greatest experience in the supply of precoated products in UK	Your problems/enquiries will be dealt with quickly and reliably

2 CATERING GRADE MARGARINE

Yellow in colour. Also available colour-free

1	Saving money	You reduce costs and remain competitive
2	Natural colours used	You can claim your cakes contain no artificial colouring and obtain a wider market
3	Traditional colour	Your production people and customers will not notice any change in your product
4	Colour option; for example, you can use white cake margarine to produce filling cream	You do not waste money on good cake of wrong colour

All vegetable oil blend

1	Vegetable oils do not go rancid as quickly as animal oils	Your cakes will have a longer shelf-life; your customers will notice the best quality right to the end of the sell-by date

Features	Benefits	'You appeal'
	2 Attractive to the large health conscious market	Your sales could increase due to the trend for healthy foods and vegetarian products
	3 Better stability	You gain consistent quality and less chance of complaint
Complex natural additives	1 High performance	Your cakes will have larger volume, allowing you to scale at a lower weight, thus giving you better profit
	2 Carry-through flavour	Your cakes will have that rich, individual traditional flavour, building brand loyalty
	3 Natural *permitted* additives	Your cakes containing this margarine will have longer shelf-life and extra sales due to its freshness right till the end of its sell-by date
	4 Fewer additives than many other margarines	You don't have to list as many additives and your sales will increase

5 Greater yield — You will be able to reduce unit cost

6 Effective as shortening at 20 per cent lower cost — You find it easier to price competitively and keep profit margin high

Packed in 0.5 kg in polythene-lined cardboard boxes and own label if required

1 Easy to handle — The ideal weight that all your staff will be able to carry without danger or complaint

2 Standardised weight — You can base your recipes on how many boxes per mix – this reduces your handling time

3 'Own label' masks your supplier — Your competitor will not know which margarine you are using, making it more difficult to match your product

4 Prevents production staff interference — You prevent your production staff noticing if you choose another supplier

Features	Benefits	'You appeal'
	5 Easily stored	Your stores manager will be pleased that each pallet holds 1 tonne of product, making it easier for stock checking and reducing loss by theft
	6 No clips or staples used	You will not have to worry about foreign bodies being found in your product
	7 Accepted by EEC + BS	You will have no problems using our product in goods made for EEC standards
Major supplier (direct or through national distributors) of oils and fats to the bakery, catering and food manufacturing industries	1 Product range available nationally	You can choose to have product direct or distributors hold stock for you

2 Very wide range — You reduce the number of suppliers you need

3 Excellent pricing structure — You reduce costs, simply by not having to pay for long distance deliveries

1 Guaranteed quality products — You reduce the risk of complaint

Have a test bakery, laboratory and full field technical supplies

2 Technical back-up — You will have at your request a full technical service team that will work with you on new product development and plant trials

3 Customers can use the facility — You and your staff can use the test bakery without disruption of your normal production

3 MICROFILM CAMERA

Features		Benefits	'You appeal'
This camera uses a system very similar to conventional processing of camera cards – no pressure is used	1	The operation of processing is cleaner	Your operators will not have to clean the tubes or aperture chamber as frequently
	2	Time saving on down-time and maintenance	You reduce delays and complaints
	3	The chamber is flooded, as opposed to chemical being forced in by pressure	Your final films will last longer with no emulsion damage to cause complaint
	4	The processing speed is the same as that of a 30 mm camera	Your operators' output will not be affected
	5	The same operator exposes and processes the film	You save on staff cost, training and equipment

This camera has an attachment on the head to provide a facility for indexing	1 Once the cards have been exposed and processed, the operator can index them as well	You reduce operator costs by one person
	2 Saving on the movement of cards from one work station to another	You eliminate the chance of incorrect indexing and subsequent complaints
The camera is completely controlled by a computer switch and all instructions are put through the computer	1 Ensuring exact reduction ratio unlike mechanical cam-operated camera	You will be giving a better quality product to your customer
	2 Standard reduction ratios or any required reduction ratio can be programmed into the computer	You reduce time, cost and reject work

Features	Benefits	'You appeal'
	3 Faults are isolated and relayed to VDU	Your operator will then be able to make corrections instead of calling an engineer
	4 The operator has complete control over the camera, making each function less of a problem for him/her	Your average job cost is reduced
The camera uses fluorescent lights	1 Does not throw out heat	You can provide better working conditions for your operators, leading to better output, without extra cost
	2 Low power consumption	You save on electricity
	3 Constant light: your operator is in a better lighted area	You reduce operator fatigue and complaints
	4 More even spread of light over the table area	You increase quality of the copy and reduce 'retake' costs

The company's stock is computer controlled

1. Extraction of information from computer easy — You can have immediate information relating to stock given to you over the phone

2. Extraction of information from computer quicker — You will be able to respond to your customer more quickly

3. The stock control system informs our people when more stock of a particular product is needed — You will find that we are rarely out of stock of the product

The company have two of their own delivery vans fitted with telephones

1. Which gives three day delivery service — You do not need to keep high levels of stock

2. Tighter control on delivery schedules — You can arrange an urgent delivery easily

3. The drivers work for the company — You obtain quicker, more flexible delivery and higher security

4 WAREHOUSE RACKING

Features	Benefits	'You appeal'
Box section beams	1 Double thickness of material at top and bottom of section	Your loading capacity is made safer
	2 Double thickness at four corners	You achieve better impact resistance and longer lasting racks
	3 Less beam deflection than open section	You reduce the chance of racks collapsing with risk of injury and stock loss
	4 Safety factor 1.65 to 1	You have a safe system even if the operators exceed maximum quoted loadings
	5 Juggled nesting 'C' sections	You have nothing for forks of truck to catch on and separate
	6 Ease of placement of rack accessories	You have a more rigid and secure rack
	7 Versatile section	You can use and fit to suit your site's needs

Each connector if fitted with six lugs, argon welded, with chrome safety lock and drainage holes	1 Lugs are cold roll formed	You increase loading capacity of rack, giving more space
	2 Better penetration and greatly reduced spatter	You gain better loading capability and neater, cleaner, safer weld
	3 Three more lugs than other suppliers provide	Your pallets impose less load per lug, reducing the chance of lug failure
	4 Because of lug design strapping is not needed	Your operators can easily move beams and therefore make better use of cubic capacity
	5 Connector bears on three faces	Your connector's 'wraparound' effect reduces dangerous side sway of rack and increases operator confidence

Features	Benefits	'You appeal'
	6 Operators can visually check for correct placement of safety lock	You reduce the chance of major accident
	7 Drainage holes reduce the build up of condensation inside the beam section, thus prolonging working life	Your rack lasts much longer
Welded end frame, checked by quality control delivered in one piece	1 Reduces installation times	You'll get into your new warehouse more quickly and save on installation costs
	2 Quicker replacement	Your warehouse operation will not be disrupted as long when replacing damaged frames
	3 Guaranteed square frame	You know all frames will fit and time will not be lost on site alterations

4	Avoidance of human error	Your installation team cannot incorrectly assemble frame on site
5	Footplate part of frame	You know the strength of the frame is alright because footplate welded on during manufacture cannot work loose
6	No sway	You eliminate movement of the frame during positioning of pallets, therefore safer and more confident operators
1	Large customer base	You will find thousands of satisfied customers in the UK and worldwide will testify to Redirack's excellence and thereby endorse your decision
	Manufacturing same basic design of rack for 25 years in UK manufacturing plant	
2	Vast experience of customer problems and applications	You can be sure we know how to offer the best solution to your requirements

Features	Benefits	'You appeal'
Direct project sales team and distributor network with all sales team and design engineers highly trained and all layout work, consultancy and guidance provided free of charge	1 Can react quickly to imminent project	You save time because our salesman and design engineer will help in quick turnaround of drawings, budget quotes and proposals
	2 Local distributor network	Your local area will have a stock-holding distributor for speedy delivery of small quantities
	3 No consultancy fees	You don't need to allocate additional budget resources

Index